Becoming a Professional LOVER

A Weekly Devotional for
Learning to Love God's Way

Claude Jr. & Jocelyn Thomas
with Patrice Thomas Conwell

ISBN 978-0-578-55024-4 (paperback)
ISBN 978-0-578-55029-9 (digital)

Copyright © 2017 by Claude Jr. & Jocelyn Thomas
Visit our website at: www.theprofessionallover.net

Copy Editor: Dr. Dorothy J.M. Patterson
Cover Design: square1studio

All rights reserved. No part of this publication may be reproduced, distributed, or transmitted in any form or by any means, including photocopying, recording, or other electronic or mechanical methods without the prior written permission of the publisher. For permission requests, solicit the publisher via the address below.

PeeTee Communications, LLC
Huntsville, Alabama 35810
www.ptcommunications.biz

Printed in the United States of America

DEDICATIONS

First, we dedicate this book to our children, their spouses, our grandchildren and great-grandchildren, because we want them to have what we have, and more. Without you, we wouldn't be who we are today with a story to tell.

Then, we dedicate this book to all couples who want to make a lasting success of their relationship, extending beyond this present life; one that will enable us all to go home with Jesus — as a family — when He comes.

Lastly, we dedicate this book to our extended families and all of the people who have become family through love and friendship. We've struggled together and shared good times, strengthening each other and lifting each other up, and we love you.

A special "Thank you" to our daughter for her faithfulness and untiring effort in telling our story to the world.

CONTENTS

Introduction 9

Week 1.	Pattern your love after Christ and His church.	15
Week 2.	Structure your love around all the principles in 1 Corinthians 13	18
Week 3.	Doing things God's way results in happiness.	21
Week 4.	Love is a commitment, not a feeling	24
Week 5.	Choose to be happy, and you will be.	27
Week 6.	Acknowledge that everyone has a personal love style.	30
Week 7.	Love isn't love until your spouse says so.	33
Week 8.	Get to know how your spouse perceives love.	36
Week 9.	Love your spouse his or her way.	39
Week 10.	Loving your spouse your way is selfish.	42
Week 11.	Respect each other's individual needs.	...45

Week 12. To love a woman, a man has to accept how she thinks. 48
Week 13. To love a man, a woman has to accept how he thinks. 51
Week 14. Don't forget–GOD made man *and* woman. 54
Week 15. Treat marriage like a partnership. 57
Week 16. Common values are vital. 60
Week 17. God says, "Two cannot walk together unless they be agreed." 63
Week 18. Oneness in harmony, not sameness, holds a marriage together. 66
Week 19. You're alike enough to understand each other. 69
Week 20. You're different enough to enrich each other. 72
Week 21. Recognize, appreciate, and use each other's skills to help love grow. 75
Week 22. Frequent words of praise keep happiness and joy alive. 78
Week 23. Daily demonstrate your love for each other. 81
Week 24. Motivate resolutions by never making divorce an option. 84
Week 25. Listen… listen… listen to each other. 87
Week 26. Respect each other's needs and ideas as important. 90
Week 27. Settle your differences by meeting each other's present needs. 93
Week 28. Never go to bed angry. 96

Week 29. Unresolved anger and resentment will destroy a marriage. 99
Week 30. Forgiveness and love will save a marriage. 102
Week 31. Togetherness in work and play will keep you bonded. 105
Week 32. Make time to have fun together. 108
Week 33. Sex is for pleasure; as well as for intimacy and creating children. 111
Week 34. Live within your means to avoid financial problems. 114
Week 35. Use credit only when *absolutely* needed. 117
Week 36. Using cash is better than credit. 120
Week 37. Budget a faithful tithe and offering to keep God's blessings flowing. 123
Week 38. Friends outside the marriage should be friends of the couple. 126
Week 39. Loyalty is to one's marriage and family. 129
Week 40. A happy home is where God-likeness reigns supreme. 132
Week 41. Remember – YOU are not the family. 135
Week 42. Don't neglect each other as you care for the children. 138
Week 43. Parent your children together. 141
Week 44. Children feel happy and secure when the parents are happy. 144
Week 45. Create family traditions to celebrate special occasions. 147

Week 46. Have morning and evening family worship. 150

Week 47. Daily Bible study together *and* alone is essential. 153

Week 48. As a wife, make Proverbs 31:10-31 your daily goal. 156

Week 49. As a husband, make Ephesians 5:25-29 your daily goal. 159

Week 50. Make God your partner, and ask Him to help you love your spouse. 162

Week 51. Recognize that love, marriage, sex, and family are God's idea — not man's. 165

Week 52. Become a professional lover through study, time, and effort. 168

INTRODUCTION

For over 40 years, we were blessed with opportunities to share our knowledge and personal experiences of marriage with couples across the United States. During that time, we began using the phrase, "professional lover."

The phrase elicited the most response from the men attending our seminars. They'd nod their heads and smile like, "Yeah, my man! He's a *professional* lover." It's an idea that attracted the men because the phrase implies being skilled in romancing women, much like a "Cassanova."

While that's definitely a part of being a professional lover, in God's eyes it's a very small part. Much smaller when compared to the other facets of loving. And to become a professional lover, you have to be skilled in *all* of love's facets; not just one or two.

Becoming a professional lover God's way is not for the faint-hearted. It will take study, practice, and time.

Think about it: What did it take for you to become a professional in your career? For many of us, it took at least four years of college built on 12 years of schooling prior to college. That equals 16 years. Then many of us added one to four years of graduate school. That equals 17 to 20 years. Some did even more. And embedded within all of those years are thousands and thousands of hours of study and practice. What a commitment!

Becoming a professional lover will take the same kind of commitment to study, practice, and proficiency. And it will not happen in a few weeks or a few months. In fact, it really is a life-long education, but an exciting one. As you begin practicing God's way of loving, its impact on others and yourself will result in rewards beyond your imagination.

As we share with you the process of becoming a professional lover, we're working on several assumptions. We assume that:

- You are *truly* interested in loving *God's* way;
- You understand that God's way *always runs counter* to man's way;
- You will guard against personal interpretation of scriptural passages by searching all related scriptures and contexts;
- You are fully able to cognitively process this information and rationally choose your behavior;
- You understand that there are exceptions to every generally-used description.

Introduction

To get the most from this devotional, we suggest that you begin each study time with prayer. You'll need the power of the Holy Spirit to discern the truth behind the principles we offer and to make you *willing and able* to practice them.

We also suggest that you use a variety of study tools, among them: A dictionary, a few different bible translations — particularly the King James Version and Amplified Bible, and a Bible concordance. This will aid you in getting the most understanding and complete knowledge from what you read.

Finally, we suggest that you have an accountability partner. It can be your spouse, best friend, or someone else reading this book who's striving to love the way God loves. Holding yourself accountable to someone else will motivate you to practice what you read.

The Bible tells us that love has meaning; love has structure; and love has style. We aim to explore all of those facets as we start you on your journey to becoming a professional lover, God's way.

love \'lev\ — satisfying the legitimate
human needs of another through
your own resources or by guiding one
into a direction where resources are found

WEEK 1

Pattern your love after Christ and His church.

"Husbands, love your wives, even as Christ also loved the church, and gave himself for it; wives submit yourselves unto your own husbands, as unto the Lord" Ephesians 5:25 & 22, KJV.

Often, people who sew use patterns; replications of the garment's pieces. You don't have to guess about how to do anything. Just pin the pattern to your fabric, cut it out, and follow the sewing instructions.

Likewise, you don't have to guess about how to love. God left us a pattern — a replication of how He loves us, preserved in the Bible.

Ephesians 5 lays out the pattern of love for us. It begins by telling us how a "follower of God" thinks and behaves versus one who does not follow Him. Then, it shows how the individual's godly behavior translates to the marriage union:

> *"Wives, submit yourselves unto your own husbands, as unto the Lord. For the husband is the head of the wife, even as Christ is the head of the church… Husbands, love your wives, even as Christ also loved the church, and gave himself for it… So ought men to love their wives as their own bodies. He that loveth his wife loveth himself" Ephesians 5: 22-23, 25 & 28, KJV.*

We purposefully inverted today's text because many focus only on the submission of wives to husbands rather than focusing equally on the pattern of love for both wives *and* husbands. Also, the thought of submission dredges up mental pictures of the misuse and abuse of male dominance that women often experience.

But if husbands love their wives the way *Christ* loves the church, wives will not hesitate to submit. Christ's love *never* involves abuse, misuse of power, selfishness, intolerance, injustice, or disrespect. In fact, He willingly gave up His life for His church.

Don't be blinded by the ways that humans distort God's love pattern to fit their own designs. When people do that, it shows that they don't have a true or complete understanding of or connection to God. And Satan loves that because it causes us to question or mistrust God.

In fact, Ephesians 5 tells us exactly what to do with people who distort God's pattern. It says don't associate with them or share with them. Instead, use your living by God's pattern as a way to expose and reprove their deception, and, hopefully, convict them to God's way (Amplified Bible).

Christ gave us a perfect love pattern because He was perfect through His Father's power. In order for imperfect people, like us, to follow Christ's pattern of love, we need His Father's — our Father's — power as well.

This week's homework:

Using an Amplified Bible, study Ephesians 5 and 1 Peter 3. Outline God's love pattern for *you* first, then for your spouse. Using the elements of love detailed in the stories of the Good Samaritan (Luke 10:25-37) and the woman caught in adultery (John 8:3-11), describe what the love pattern should look like in day-to-day living.

WEEK 2

Structure your love around all the principles in 1 Corinthians 13.

"And now abideth faith, hope, charity, these three; but the greatest of these is charity" 1 Corinthians 13:13, KJV.

Remember our sewing example from last week? Using a pattern takes all of the guesswork out of creating a garment.

Once all of the garment pieces are cut out, you can begin structuring the garment by sewing all of the pieces together.

It's the same with love. Once you have the pattern of love, you can begin putting all of the pieces together.

1 Corinthians 13:4-8 details all of love's pieces that, once put together, provide the perfect structure of love:

- It endures long and is patient and kind;
- It never envies nor boils over with jealousy;
- It does not boast or say, "Look at me";
- It is not conceited or arrogant;
- It is not rude or unbecoming in behavior;
- It does not insist on its own way;
- It isn't touchy, fretful or resentful;
- It doesn't keep count of wrongs;
- It doesn't rejoice at injustice;
- It doesn't fade out or come to an end.

Wow! If we truly loved each other and our spouses according to these principles, think of the number of relationships and marriages that would not end.

But the reality is that they do end. And why? Because we don't behave by all of these principles all of the time. While some of these principles are inherently easy for us to conform to, based on our personalities and our strengths, others are extremely difficult. But that's not a good enough reason to not do them all.

God expects us to cultivate the necessary skills to behave by all of these principles of love. And we have to learn *how* to use each, *when* to use each, and *the degree* to which to use each in every situation that we encounter. Difficult? Yes! Impossible? No! Not with God's help every step of the way.

This week's homework:

Using the Amplified Bible and a dictionary, study each love principle, looking up specific words and the various other adjectives used for those words. Write out a description of what each principle means. Then, determine which of those principles align — right now — within your strengths and which ones fall within your weaknesses. Choose one principle that you're weak in that is greatly hindering the success of your marital relationship. Begin praying over that principle, asking God to change your desire and ability to behave by that principle.

WEEK 3

Doing things God's way results in happiness.

"If ye know these things, happy are ye if ye do them" John 13:17, KJV.

I can imagine that by now, many of you might be wondering if God's way of loving is even possible for us to do. If you're thinking it isn't, you're right.

Because our natural selves are slaves to sin (Romans 7:21-25), it's impossible for us to love according to the pattern and structure you've studied over the last two weeks. We can *only* do it in God's power.

If we choose to love God's way, He guarantees that we will experience a level of happiness that surpasses anything we've ever known. But how are we defining "happiness"?

Many people define happiness as a feeling of excitement or satisfaction that results from things going our way. When we feel positive, we're happy. When we feel good, we're happy. If we have no complaints, we're happy.

But what happens when things are not going our way? Or what happens when we do have something to complain about? Or we're feeling negatively? Then we say we're not happy! Which means that our happiness depends on the *specific instances* that we encounter in life that make us *feel* good. That's not God's definition of happy.

In Matthew 5, Jesus outlines what true happiness is. Although the word used is "blessed," the Amplified Bible adds the adjectives, "happy, to be envied, and spiritually prosperous-with life-joy and satisfaction in God's favor and salvation, *regardless of their outward conditions.*"

God's definition of "happy" is satisfaction that comes from knowing that we have God's favor and salvation because we're doing what *God* asks us to do. It is not a physical state of feeling; it's a spiritual state of assurance.

This actually falls within one dictionary definition of happiness as, "a state of well-being and contentment." If you look up the word "state," one meaning is, "a way of living or existing." So if we love according to God's pattern and structure, our entire existence will be one of well-being and contentment — or, happiness.

Thank goodness that doing things God's way often produces a physical state of happiness, as well. God does want us to feel good, but right now, sin relegates that to specific instances. As human beings, God knows that we need those specific instances as a way to grow our faith that His design actually works.

As our faith grows, so will our state of happiness, because we know — through our spiritual assurance — that one day, salvation will allow our spiritual and physical happiness to always exist together.

This week's homework:

Using several bibles and a bible concordance, look up the words *happy* and *happiness* and write down how each scripture describes what it means to be happy.

WEEK 4

Love is a commitment, not a feeling.

"Herein is love, not that we loved God, but that he loved us, and sent his Son to be the propitiation for our sins. Beloved, if God so loved us, we ought also to love one another" 1 John 4:10 & 11, KJV.

We heard a preacher tell the story of one of his members who came to him for counseling with her mind made up to divorce her husband. The preacher asked her to wait for three months. During those three months, she was to love her husband following the pattern in Ephesians 5 and 1 Peter 3.

When she came back after the three months, the preacher asked her, "Shall we go ahead with your plan to divorce your husband?"

"Oh no," she responded with force. "Divorce him for what? He's wonderful and is treating me like a princess."

What made the difference?

All of the traits and behavior of her husband that drove her to the brink of divorce changed through her loving him God's way. The love that she *chose* to give produced in him a love for her that she could actually experience.

That's the essence of today's text. Jesus did not wait for us to love Him. He did not take on our sin and die for us because we loved Him. He loved us first. And He died for us because He loved us first.

In return, when we grasp the magnitude of Jesus' sacrifice for us, we love Him (1 John 4:19). And He feels our love through our obedience.

God knows that it's easy to love someone who returns love to us. He says if you love only the people who love you, what kind of reward is that? Everybody does that (Matthew 5:46). But if you love your enemies, then you're really doing something.

While we wouldn't consider a spouse or a friend an enemy, sometimes he or she acts in ways that make us feel the same way an enemy does. And sometimes, we act the same way toward them. At those times, lovey-dovey feelings disappear, and if they're gone too long, our very desire to love disappears, as well.

That's where commitment should take over. The foundation of how we love is built on choice, not on feelings. It comes from our commitment to God to love another the way He says to.

And here's the beauty: if we exhibit faith in God's design, it releases His power to work on our behalf. So that how a person feels loved by us will evoke the same type of love in response to us.

Then what happens? The feeling and desire come back and stay because we're both loving each other God's way.

This week's homework:

Find and write the meaning of *commitment* that relates to getting the job done. Then, list several things from your individual experience related to your education, your job, a hobby, or an interest that you've been committed to in the past. Analyze how you behaved when you didn't *feel* like completing it, and compare that to how you behave in your relationship.

WEEK 5

Choose to be happy, and you will be.

"He that handleth a matter wisely shall find good: and whoso trusteth in the Lord, happy is he" Proverbs 16:20, KJV.

Jo and I were conducting a marriage seminar at a church in Detroit, Michigan. During one of the afternoon sessions, she was with the wives in one room, and I was with the husbands in a separate room.

All of a sudden, I heard a roar of discontent and angry words and grunts erupt from her area. It was so loud and contentious that I almost left my group to make sure she wasn't being torn apart, limb from limb.

Later, I discovered that the ruckus broke out after she'd read to them 1 Peter 3:1, where Peter admonishes wives to submit themselves to their husbands in a meek and gentle manner, where their conversation would convert their husbands, even if they weren't believers.

First of all, you know that the general feeling of women concerning submission is not positive. Couple that with telling women to subject themselves to husbands who are not making them happy, and you have the scenario that Jo experienced.

Yet, when one is *not* feeling happy is precisely when you must *choose* to be happy. If the household atmosphere is positive and light-hearted, you don't have to choose to be happy. It already promotes happiness.

So why should you choose to be happy in the face of negativity, and how do you do that?

First, remember that in Week 3 we defined "happiness" as a state of existing in contentment, and not specific instances of feeling good. So when you choose to be happy, you're choosing to live in contentment, even when the overall atmosphere doesn't promote good feelings.

Second, "choosing" requires action. You must actively make a choice to live contentedly because you made the commitment to marry and stay married — and commitment is a principle, as we discussed last week.

Third, you choose to be happy because God asks you to. This is evident in His pattern and structure of love. It's also evident in 1 Peter 3:10 & 11, where God says, "For he that will love life, and see good days, let him refrain his tongue from evil, and his lips that they speak no guile; Let him eschew evil, and do good; let him seek peace, and ensue it," KJV.

So how *does* one choose to be happy? First, think back on times when positivity flowed back and forth between you and your spouse, and focus on those. Second, ask God for His power to feel content, and pray for the situation — or your spouse — that may be sowing seeds of discontent. This gives God the opportunity to move on both your hearts in order to redeem the relationship.

Finally, remember that doing the right thing, in the right way, at the right time, to the right degree, for the right reason, will produce predictable results. I call this the science of redemption. When you do this, God guarantees that *He* will bring about a new spirit. All you need to do is trust Him to do it.

This week's homework:

Read the entire chapter of 1 Peter 3. As you read, outline all the ways God expects us to react in good *and* bad times.

WEEK 6

Acknowledge that everyone has a personal love style.

"He that saith, I know him, and keepeth not his commandments, is a liar, and the truth is not in him" 1 John 2:4, KJV.

I awoke before daybreak one morning to find that Claude (or "Jackie" as he's known to family) was not in bed. I found him at the kitchen table sitting motionless, head in his hands.

"Honey, are you okay?" I asked.

Silence. He didn't even move to look at me.

"Honey," I said with more concern. "What's the matter? Are you okay?"

Acknowledge that everyone has a personal love style

"You don't love me," he replied.

Knowing I'd heard him wrong I responded with a little chuckle, "Okay, stop playing. What's wrong?"

"In fact," he continued, "You've *never* loved me!"

Instantly, the ten years that we'd been married flashed through my mind. Tears sprang into my eyes and the sting of his words bubbled up from my soul as I thought of a laundry list of ways I could angrily tick off, one-by-one, examples of how I had, indeed, given him all of my love.

But something else within me "stomped down" that instant reaction and I told myself, "Be quiet. You need to listen to him."

He explained to me that the loving style test he had taken showed that while I was loving him hard, I wasn't loving *him*. His test results gave voice to the frustration he'd felt throughout our marriage — a frustration I never even sensed or knew existed.

Each of us perceives love a different way. Based on our personalities and the cultures and environments in which we grew up, we all have our own interpretations of what makes us feel loved. It's not about right or wrong; it just is.

Even God has a love style. John 4:21 says, "Whoever has my commands and keeps them is the one who loves me…" KJV. And our text this week says that if we say we love God but don't keep His commandments, then we're lying.

Those are strong words! The way that God feels loved is through our obedience. If we don't obey His commandments, then we're not behaving in ways that satisfy His needs. Thus, we're lying when we say we love Him but don't obey Him. This is the style that God's love pattern and pieces ultimately result in.

How important it is, then, to know whom you're loving. With that information, we can see more clearly how to use each other's style within the love pattern, taking the way that we love to the next level.

This week's homework:

Discover your love style by taking a test, such as the one associated with John Lee's *Colors of Love* or Gary Chapman's *Five Love Languages*. Note the commonalities and differences between your and your spouse's styles.

WEEK 7

Love isn't love until your spouse says so.

"And let us consider one another to provoke unto love and to good works" Hebrews 10:24, KJV.

Loving your spouse in his or her love style takes discipline and patience. Our natural inclination is to love another in our own way, especially when we believe that what we're doing is good or benefits another.

Jo is a "doer." Her primary loving style is more in line with agape love. She loves through serving others. So when I, or we, would come home from work, she'd start bustling around the kitchen to get dinner ready. After dinner, she was bustling around the house doing this and that. She was always busy, serving me and our family.

While there is nothing "wrong" with that, my primary loving style is friendship love. I feel loved through togetherness — spending time sitting and talking, or sharing common interests, or just being together in the same room. But to get her to sit was nearly impossible.

While I understood that five children and a house to manage required a lot of work, sometimes I'd have to say, "Jo, that's enough. I can do that myself."

Her service, particularly for me, was out of balance; she didn't know when to stop, or even that she *could* stop. And all of her bustling around was not making me feel loved. I wanted *time* with her, not her service.

Doesn't that sound vaguely familiar to the biblical story of Martha in Luke 10:38-42? Martha, the "doer" who was always busy working for others, became annoyed with her sister, Mary, who was sitting — spending time with Jesus.

Martha began fussing because she felt Mary should have been helping her. Which means that what she really wanted was for Mary to love Jesus her way.

When Martha asked Jesus to rebuke Mary and make her get up and help, Jesus gently rebuked Martha instead. He let her know that Mary had her own needs which were just as important as Martha's. And to Jesus, if one had to choose between spending time *with* Him and working *for* Him, time with Him was the better choice in loving Jesus His way.

Each of us can point out what makes our own love style important or necessary for another. But really, it's necessary for ourselves. In contrast, God's love style is selfless. And ultimately, our personal love styles are superseded by His. That means that if we love the way God loves, we will work to love each other in the ways that *the other* feels loved.

This week's homework:

Now that you know your love style and your partner's love style, sit together and discuss where your styles differ and where they're similar. Think about, and cite examples, of how you've seen those similarities and differences displayed in your daily behaviors and interactions.

WEEK 8

....

Get to know how your spouse perceives love.

"Study to shew thyself approved unto God, a workman that needeth not to be ashamed, rightly dividing the word of truth" 2 Timothy 2:15, KJV.

The wife of one couple we counseled felt extremely frustrated that nothing she did seemed to make her husband happy. She was very confused and hurt by his negative responses, or lack of responses of any kind. So we asked her, "What are you doing when your husband seems the happiest?"

She began reciting a few things, after which we asked her husband, "What things about your wife make you happy?"

As he began to share with her and with us, she would periodically respond with an astonished, "I didn't know that!"

In order to love each other in the ways that make us feel loved, we have to study each other. What does that mean? Expounding on today's text, the Amplified Bible says that it means, "correctly analyzing and accurately dividing [rightly handling and skillfully teaching]… Truth."

Though Paul was admonishing Timothy about the correct way to share with others the truth about God, the same principle applies in this context. Through intentional, careful observation and discussion — for accurate information — you should learn what behaviors elicit both positive *and* negative responses from your spouse.

And then, how do we "rightly handle" the truth? In our context, it means creating an environment that makes discussion productive. Talk together at a time and in a place where emotions and thoughts are healthy and neutral. Listen and respond without judgment or condemnation. You should feel safe opening yourselves up to each other.

Paul also tells Timothy that he should "*be eager and do your utmost* to present yourself to God approved [tested by trial]…" In other words, Timothy was to excitedly do everything in his power to show God that he knew the Word of Truth in theory (study) *and* practice (tested by trial) before sharing it with others.

Likewise, we should eagerly want to learn about *and* practice the behaviors that make our spouses feel loved. Doing so falls in line with God's love style and pattern.

This week's homework:

Continuing your discussion from last week, ask each other what behaviors demonstrate your love styles. Ask, "Is there anything that I currently do that makes you feel loved? What else should I do to love you the way you need to be loved?" If necessary, write your spouse's answers down so you can see them and commit them to memory.

WEEK 9

Love your spouse his or her way.

"If ye love me, keep my commandments"
John 14:15, KJV.

Once Jo's and my love styles were clear to each other, the work of learning how to satisfy each other's love needs began. And it still continues, even though we've been married over 50 years. Meeting each other's love needs requires constant thinking and retraining your thoughts and behaviors every day. Because our own love style is automatic, it's hard to think in someone else's style all the time.

How could Jo bridge her need "to do" with my need "for time" with her? How could I bridge my need "for time" with her need "to do" for me? We had to find ways to integrate the two. Often, that meant while she cooked, I cleaned; or, I would sit in the kitchen with her and chat. On the flip side, often after making my dinner plate, she'd keep my food hot while she made her own so we could eat together.

There's no cut-off time or point at which we've filled a quota when it comes to loving each other in the way that we each need. Is there ever a time when God is finished meeting our needs? Lamentations 3:23 says that God's compassions for us are new *every* morning.

But what happens if a spouse's love style is negative or unhealthy? Or what happens if only one person is actively trying to meet the other's love needs but is not getting his or hers met in return?

First, we believe that a love style itself is not unhealthy, but how the style is practiced might be. For instance, a person who needs words of affirmation might display that need through making you "prove" your love, whether through aggressive demands, or by always playing the victim.

If that's the case, remember that the standard to reach is God's love pattern and the love pieces we've already discussed. If the behaviors don't meet the standard, do whatever is necessary to bring them in line, even if it means getting third-party help from a trusted, Christian professional.

Second, our ultimate commitment to love is to God. We follow God's love pattern — not because we're getting it in return — but because that's what

He asked us to do. And He says, if we love *Him*, we will *choose* to obey Him. We know at times it's hard to love others who aren't loving us in return, but we also know that God will give us what we need to help us obey Him.

This week's homework:

From the list that you wrote last week of behaviors that demonstrate your spouse's love needs, commit to doing one thing every day that makes your spouse feel loved.

WEEK 10

Loving your spouse your way is selfish.

"And when they came to Nachon's threshingfloor, Uzza put forth his hand to the ark of God, and took hold of it; for the oxen shook it. And the anger of the Lord was kindled against Uzza; and God smote him there for his error; and there he died by the ark of God" 2 Samuel 6:6 & 7, KJV.

The wife of a couple with whom we're friends planned a huge surprise birthday party for her husband who had never had one. She went to great lengths and expense for his big shindig.

When she sprang it on him, he was furious. And his reaction hurt his bewildered wife. After all that she had done for him, he was angry instead of happy! Why?

He'd told her many times that he did not like surprises. But she felt that because a birthday party was a good surprise, it would make him feel special. Instead, he felt disregarded.

Usually we would not consider ourselves "selfish" if our ways of loving are directed toward someone else and are not intended to harm. But, think about the story of Uzza.

From the time the ark of the covenant was built, God instructed that human hands were not to touch it. It was God's dwelling place; therefore, it was holy. When the Israelites moved from camp-to-camp, the priests carried the ark by poles inserted in holders located on each corner of the ark.

Once David began reigning as king over all of Israel, he went to retrieve the ark and bring it back to Judah. They put it on a cart, and when the rough ride caused the ark to tip, Uzza instinctively reached out and grabbed it to keep it from falling. Instantly, he died.

David got angry with God for punishing Uzza so harshly. After all, wasn't Uzza looking out for the ark? Weren't his intentions noble? On the face of it, we would agree with David. But when you think about it, we can understand God's point.

God was *very specific* about how to transport His dwelling place. David was so eager to have the ark back with him that he allowed his good intentions to blind him. He didn't think about God's directions. First mistake.

Then, David assumed that God would accept, and honor, his — and Uzza's — good intentions. Second mistake. It was not David's place to assume something different than what he'd already been told.

Don't we still do that to God today? Many times, instead of obeying God in the ways He's asked us to, we obey Him in ways that make us feel good, or that we interpret as good, or in ways that are convenient for us. And then we get angry when He doesn't honor our obedience. Our *selfish* obedience.

Once we know what our spouse's love needs are and the specific behaviors that demonstrate it, God expects us to accept and honor them.

This week's homework:

Ask your spouse, "What do I do that does *not* make you feel loved?" Without being defensive, listen and write down the answers. Ask God to "prick" your memory when you're behaving in ways that your spouse says are unloving. Ask Him for the strength to change. And ask your spouse to pray for you, as well.

WEEK 11

Respect each other's individual needs.

Be kindly affectioned one to another with brotherly love; in honour preferring one another" Romans 12:10, KJV.

For many people, it's hard to distinguish between a need and a want. Societal values and norms have altered our ability to truly discern what is essential to our existence. But if we go back to God's word, it shows us how to tell the difference.

Let's consider the story of creation. God's ultimate desire was to create beings in His image. But man was not the first thing He created. He, first, created everything that man needed to survive and grow.

God created an appropriate environment to sustain man — light, air, water, land, and food. Then, God created an environment to give him a sense of responsibility and fulfillment — creatures of water and air and land animals.

Once God set up everything, *then* He created Adam and put him to work, to stimulate his creativity and thinking. While Adam was working, he noticed that every animal had another of its kind, but he, himself, didn't. When he mentioned it to God, God agreed that Adam needed a "help meet," a companion to support him and share life with him. So He created Eve.

Finally, God created a specific time for Adam and Eve to rest from their everyday work and to focus solely on His blessings to — and His love for — them.

When you pay close attention to this account, you get a sense of what defines a need. A need is something that is essential to life and growth. It's something that you can't do without. God's order of actions said, you can't do without things that sustain you physically; you can't do without things that sustain you mentally; you can't do without things that sustain you emotionally; and you can't do without things that sustain you spiritually. Otherwise, you will not grow or continue to exist.

Because we're individuals, our needs differ within these areas. That's where respect comes in.

Sin destroyed the perfect balance of need fulfillment that God masterfully designed. We all grew up in relationships, surroundings, and cultures that supplied our needs in varying degrees.

Because of this, you will have needs that others don't, and vice versa. And instead of using your lack of need in one area as a standard for someone else, God says you have the responsibility to do everything that you can to supply someone else's need. Whether you can personally fill it, or supply other resources that can.

That is the essence of God's love toward us and our love toward each other.

This week's homework:

Look up Maslow's Hierarchy of Needs and ask your spouse how completely each one is being met. Ask whether there is anything you can do to help fulfill each need, and make notes of the answers. But remember to incorporate a biblical perspective in your discussion so that God's standards provide the correct context for behavior.

WEEK 12

To love a woman, a man has to accept how she thinks.

"Likewise, ye husbands, dwell with them according to knowledge, giving honour unto the wife…" 1 Peter 3:7, KJV.

Women thrive on conversation; most men do not unless they have a sanguine personality. Jo is a woman AND sanguine — a double whammy.

I, on the other hand, am neither. I am a thinker. I use observation and mental processing to determine what I want to say. Often, that leads to me taking my time to respond to questions. In fact, many who know me consider my "long pauses" as one of my identifying characteristics.

You can imagine how challenging this particular difference between us has been throughout our years together. In the early years of our marriage, my poor wife (not sure if I'd heard her or not) would repeat the question, and get frustrated at my lack of immediate response. How did we overcome that?

Once I started taking the time to learn about her, I began to understand that her desire for us to "talk" came out of some need that she had and wanted filled, a need that I didn't have. My job was to recognize, pinpoint, and accept whatever was driving her need to talk, and to respond in ways that satisfied her. That put my focus squarely on her and took it off of me — which is what I'm supposed to do if I'm loving her properly.

But it didn't happen overnight. It took quite some time. Through my personality style, I've only felt most comfortable talking when I'm teaching or lecturing. To this day, I very seldom engage in "small talk." But to love Jo in her way, I've had to force myself to converse *with* her; to actively listen to her, and to respond appropriately. As a result, I've seen her frustration decrease, which makes me feel happy and encourages our love.

When God made Eve, He made her differently from Adam. He shaped her *out of* Adam, which implies that — being suitable for him — she had a lot in common with Adam to allow them to work well together. But at the same time, because God did not make another Adam, you'd expect that there were significant differences between them.

It's the same for us. Instead of being frustrated by each other's differences, we can utilize them to enrich each other's lives.

This week's homework:

Take some time to list, study and make notes of the physiological and emotional ways that women differ from men. Stay away from trivializing them in terms of stereotypes. Use other resources that focus on these differences (e.g. Mark Gungor's *Tale of Two Brains*, John Gray's *Men are from Mars; Women are from Venus*, or Shaunti Feldhahn's *For Men Only* and *For Women Only*). Determine the degrees to which you, or your wife, exhibit those differences.

WEEK 13

To love a man, a woman has to accept how he thinks.

"All things are lawful for me, but all things are not expedient: all things are lawful for me, but all things edify not" 1 Corinthians 10:23, KJV.

Jackie is not a talker. He is known, among our family and close friends, for his "pregnant pauses." I can ask him a question, and there's silence for what seems like an eternity. I'm not even sure if he heard me, although I'm standing right next to him.

I'm the exact opposite. My mind is on speed dial all the time. Often, I tend to anticipate what someone is saying or going to say, and I'll jump in with an answer or a question. Many times Jackie, or my children will say, "Let me get the question out," or "That's not what I was going to say. Just listen!"

To say the least, my husband's tendency to take his time to answer my questions and my tendency to pepper him with questions have led to some frustrating moments for me through our years. How did we overcome that?

When I decided to marry Jackie, I loved him right away. He was a gift to me from the Lord. When you receive a gift that delights you, you take special care of it and do all you can to get the most out of it. As such, with my gift of Jackie, I had to know him specifically. I had to learn what makes him happy, what makes him tick.

Part of loving my gift meant accepting the fact that he's a good speaker in public, but he's not a verbalizer in private. And I asked the Lord to help me learn how to deal with that, and other differences, because He's the one who gave Jackie to me as a gift. I studied our gender and personality differences *and* our commonalities so I could learn how to best utilize both, in order to love him in a way that made him the best he could be.

When I took the different tests we now give to others, I discovered things about my sanguine self that I couldn't see through other people's eyes. As a result, I made changes in myself to love Jackie in his way. I had to tell myself to "Hush; don't speak now. Give him time to process what's been said. Be patient."

Even now, I still lose the reins sometimes and I have to pull back and harness myself. But it's worth it, because my frustration has decreased, which encourages our love.

God made Adam from the ground; He made Eve from Adam. They weren't even created the same way, which reflects that God intended for man and woman to be different. Yet, even though they were different, they were suitable for each other. That means that instead of viewing differences as a negative, we should view them as complimentary, and treat them as such.

This week's homework:

Using the same resources as last week, list, study, and make notes of the physiological and emotional ways that men differ from women. Again, stay away from trivializing them in terms of stereotypes. Determine the degrees to which you, or your husband, exhibit those differences.

WEEK 14

Don't forget–GOD made man *and* woman.

"So God created man in his own image, in the image of God created he him; male and female created he them" Genesis 1:27, KJV.

When you buy a car, it comes with a manual from the people who designed and created it. The manual tells you how the car is made, how it functions, and how to best care for it so that it runs a long time.

If you decide to disregard the manual and do things the way you think is best, or the way someone else tells you, you run the risk of severely damaging the way the car functions, or ruining it altogether.

God, who designed and created man *and* woman, gave us a manual that describes how we were made, how we function, and how best to maintain our relationship with each other.

As we read the account in Genesis 1 and 2, this is what we know:

- Adam and Eve were created using different methods: he from the ground, she from him.
- God blew his breath into Adam, imbuing him with God-like qualities that Adam could develop; God formed Eve from Adam's rib, giving her attributes common with and suitable for him.
- God made Adam first and gave him a job. When Adam noticed all the animals partnered up except him, God said that it wasn't good for him to be alone. He needed emotional connection.
- God made Eve as a "help meet" *for* Adam: to live, to work, and to enjoy with him the home God had created for them.
- Adam and Eve functioned alike in some aspects but differently in others so that they fit together.

It's clear that God intentionally designed and created men and women with gender commonalities *and* differences. Gender commonalities are necessary for us to be suited for one another. Gender differences are necessary for us to complement each other. This design mirrors how the Godhead operates together.

The Bible's account does *not* support that men and women are exactly the same. God did not want it that way. He designed men to think and act male; He designed women to think and act female.

The Bible's account also does *not* support that our differences warrant different treatment. Men and women have equal value in God's eyes because *He* made us both. As such, we should treat each other as having equal worth.

If you choose to follow God's manual for His creation, He promises to help you get the same relationship results as with His original design.

This week's homework:

With prayerful and honest accountability, list any beliefs and behaviors that you've adopted which devalue gender differences. Discuss them with your spouse and how they impact your relationship. Pray for each other that God will affect any necessary changes and that you will allow Him to do so.

WEEK 15

Treat marriage like a partnership.

"I pray for them...which thou hast given me...;
That they all may be one; as thou, Father,
art in me, and I in thee, that they also may
be one in us..." John 17:9 & 21, KJV.

When Jackie and I first started conducting marriage and family seminars in various churches, I began the session by sharing information about us and our family with the audience.

Jackie would then start the topic of discussion. Every so often, I would signal that I wanted to say something. He would let me speak and then just continue where he'd left off as though I hadn't said anything. His actions made me feel very insignificant and unvalued — as though what I'd said didn't matter.

I finally confronted him about my feelings and he was instantly empathetic. "Wow," he said, "that must be an awful feeling."

"Yes it is," I responded. "I know that you have all the book knowledge, but *I've* experienced everything *with* you, which is just as valuable. After all, we *are* partners!"

Recognizing his error, he worked on demonstrating that my perspective was of equal value to his own. When I'd make comments in our seminars, he would stand back and let me take the lead. Then he would acknowledge my comments by saying something like, "That was a good point, Jo." Or he would ask the women in the audience, "How do you feel about what she's saying?" He also started calling me his partner.

Many read God's pronouncement in Genesis 3 that Adam would rule over Eve and the submission principle in Ephesians 5 as God sanctioning male domination. As a result, abusive beliefs and behaviors of men have devalued the intellect, function, and roles of women in ways that devalue their worth.

In return, women have fought back by trying to erase the differences between genders, their functions, and roles, often asserting dominance as well. Both practices misrepresent God's design.

The Godhead functions in a hierarchy. God tells His Son what He wants, Jesus, gives the command, and the Holy Spirit makes it tangible. No one dictates to the other, neither do any move alone. All are consulted for making decisions, and all work together, each in His role.

After the fall, God made Adam the primary provider and the spiritual leader of the family, simulating the role of Jesus as our Intercessor. From God's design of Eve's body to nurture, grow, and bear children, she became the primary caregiver. Both still equal in value, each with different roles.

If we put all of this together, the Bible is clear that God considers men and women of equal value: both with valuable perspectives that need to be shared *and* considered in order to have full clarity of any issue.

This week's homework:

On a piece of paper, write your definitions of partnership and submission and detail what that looks like. Compare your views with your spouse's. Then, both of you study the Bible's views on submission and partnership. Talk about where your views need to change to align with the Bible's view and how you can begin the process.

WEEK 16

Common values are vital.

"For they that are after the flesh do mind the things of the flesh; but they that are after the Spirit the things of the Spirit" Romans 8:5, KJV.

When I was single, I evaluated the "husband potential" of each guy that I dated. I examined whether or not he exhibited qualities that were important to me, like the importance of family.

I grew up in a very close-knit family, one that worshipped together, played together, and traveled together. My parents enjoyed being with my brother and me, and we enjoyed being with them. My father took care of the family, working outside of the home;

my mother took care of the family, working inside of the home.

With this as my background, I wanted a man who also valued family as important, a man who wanted children, who was tender and caring, and who could provide for a family. These were core values for me, and any young man who didn't consider family togetherness just as important, didn't receive my continued attention.

We base our thoughts and behaviors on our values; they help us determine what we accept and what we reject. We have spiritual values, like our relationship to God, honesty, and respect for life, and societal/cultural values like education, ambition, and financial stability.

Thus, common values are vital to a productive relationship. They are the oil that helps make all the pieces work together smoothly. The more values that a couple have in common, the easier it is to manage the marriage relationship. The fewer values in common, the harder to manage.

This is why dating couples need to be individually clear on the values each regards as necessary to exist in a relationship *before* entering into marriage. If too many differences in your individual values exist, it suggests that the relationship might not succeed.

And don't make the mistake of assuming that your strong love for each other will change those differences after marriage. Values are not easily changed, especially by anyone other than yourself.

If you're already married and have found that you have few values in common, what happens then? Our text this week indicates how to handle that issue. If both of you value God's Word above everything else — and your marriage second — then you have a starting place from which to create commonality.

Also, focus more on the values that you have in common and less on how you differ, basing your behavior on that which you agree. And if you accept what you study in God's Word, He will see to it that you are brought together so that you can better manage your relationship.

For this week's homework:

Individually, list all of the values that you consider important. Together, compare your lists to determine commonalities and differences. Read Galatians 5:22 and 23 and discuss how the values that God sees as most important to a relationship can help you manage your differences.

WEEK 17

God says, "Two cannot walk together unless they be agreed."

"Be ye not unequally yoked together with unbelievers: for what fellowship hath righteousness with unrighteousness? and what communion hath light with darkness?" 2 Corinthians 6:14, KJV.

American society values "freedom." Americans fight for the right to express themselves freely, to make decisions freely, to worship freely, to make money freely, and to be the individual each chooses to be — freely: you do you; I'll do me.

While nothing is wrong with freedom in and of itself, as Christians our freedom is not supposed to overtake our concern for and service to each other. Nor should it ever supersede God's value system. But often, our cultural values become the standard by which we gauge our perspectives and decisions, even spiritual ones. And this is one reason people make poor relationship decisions.

It's a deceptive practice of Satan to make people believe that if they simply respect each other's freedoms, they don't have to really have common values, especially spiritual values. But God says that ultimately, that can't work.

The reality is that when people do not walk in agreement, someone is compromising in order to "keep the peace," or to make the other feel comfortable. And eventually, this weakens a relationship rather than strengthening it.

How does this happen?

The one who is willing to compromise *the least* has the greater power in a relationship. At some point, the one compromising the most will begin to resent the other or get tired of following the other. This breeds discontent that will usually seep out in words and/or behavior.

Also, when a husband and wife operate separately, i.e. you have your friends, I have mine; you have your church, I have mine — you're missing the fullness of the whole marriage package that God intended for you to have.

While many use this week's text to support a common spiritual value system, it also applies to various cultural values, as well. Differences in religious

God says, "Two cannot walk together unless they be agreed."

or spiritual beliefs and practices, as well as differences in educational, career or financial goals, relationship goals, or raising children can all cause serious problems if "unequally yoked." But *nothing* will succeed at its potential without mutual agreement with God's values.

God admonished Adam and Eve to stay *together* because their togetherness would heighten both their enjoyment AND ability to withstand temptation. He wants no less for us.

This week's homework:

Using last week's list of values, discuss your perspective on each difference of values, and whether or not you can find common ground to turn the differences into agreement. Detail what that will look like in practice. Pray together, for each other, asking God to help you change each difference into agreement, one by one.

WEEK 18

Oneness in harmony, not sameness, holds a marriage together.

"And the glory which thou gavest me I have given them; that they may be one, even as we are one" John 17:22, KJV.

Last week, we discussed how vital it is for a couple to agree with each other in order to produce a strong marital bond. But many times, people misconstrue agreement as seeing and doing everything the same way, which usually means "MY" way. That couldn't be further from the truth.

Oneness in harmony, not sameness, holds a marriage together

In Week 15, Jo related a story about how my ignoring her perspective in our seminars made her feel insignificant and unvalued. Although I was not intentionally trying to make her feel that way, my natural tendency was to focus only on *my* knowledge and *my* skill developed over time. I needed her to confront me about my tendency in order to sensitize me to valuing her views, as well.

This highlights something that every couple experiences throughout marriage: the old, "you squeeze the toothpaste in the middle and I squeeze it from the end" cliché. When people get married, we each bring to the union our own ways of doing or resolving things.

Many times, these differences cause couples to "bump heads," with each trying to convince the other that "my way" is better. The harder our heads bump, the more hurt and pain that result. Unfortunately, many couples get caught in this vicious cycle.

How can you break free?

First, ask yourself, "Is this a matter of value or style?" While it's important to have the same values, it's not necessarily important to have the same style. If we both value not being wasteful, then we'll both make sure to get every ounce of toothpaste out of the tube. HOW we each do that is a matter of style. If you prefer starting in the middle of the tube, even though it makes more sense to me to just start at the end, so what? Either way, we'll both use the entire tube of toothpaste before throwing it away.

That's the difference between value and style.

God did not create two Adams or two Eves because He didn't want two of the same. He purposefully wanted one different from the other, to mirror the harmonious interdependence of the Godhead. Harmony means being in one accord with values and goals, with both working together to move each other in the same direction.

If you seem to bicker often, or have continual arguments or disagreements, you need to ask yourselves — and one another — what is at the root of our bickering? A difference in value or style? If the values are different, we've given you the prescription for finding agreement. If the styles are different, we've given you the prescription for finding acceptance.

Remember, whether it's an issue of value or style, using God's way can serve as the basis of agreement all the time.

This week's homework:

With your partner, identify issues that you seem to disagree on or argue about too often. Determine if it's a difference of value or style. If it's a difference in value, use last week's homework to bring you into agreement. If it's a difference in style, revisit homework assignments from weeks six through 15.

WEEK 19

You're alike enough to understand each other.

"And Adam said, This is now bone of my bones, and flesh of my flesh: she shall be called Woman, because she was taken out of Man" Genesis 2:23, KJV.

We've talked a lot about the need for a couple to have commonalities in order to create a strong marital bond. When Adam didn't see any commonality between himself and the animals, he noted that to God, who then created another of his kind to support and work with him. The more you have in common, the easier it is to work together.

Because people are complex, marriage cannot be an exact science. For this reason, I'm a huge proponent of pre-marital testing. Testing gives you a tangible picture of yourself and your spouse. It shows you where you match up and where you differ. Knowing that helps you predict where relationship pitfalls may occur and how to avoid or work through them.

The loving style test that you took during Week 6 is one of three tests that I use on couples. The others are a personality test, such as the Myers-Briggs and a spiritual gifts test. In my practice, I found that the most suited couples were those who had the same elements in one or more of the tests taken.

For instance, Jo and I have the same elements in our loving styles, although they're arranged differently. My loving styles are Togetherness, High Standards, Romance, and Unselfishness. Jo's loving styles are Unselfishness, High Standards, Romance, and Togetherness. The fact that we both have the same elements helps us understand each other's needs better than if we had none in common.

And what about that? What if you discover in pre-marital testing that you have *nothing* in common? I have counseled couples not to marry. If they insisted on marrying, I would not marry them. Many who married anyway ended up divorcing. Those who listened to my counsel didn't marry.

If you're already married and discover through testing that you have very little in common, does it mean that your marriage is doomed? Absolutely not. But you have to be willing, committed, and dedicated to adapting to your spouse's needs — just as a parent does with a baby.

Even though Jo didn't feel like getting up to breastfeed at 3 a.m., or I didn't enjoy changing a stinky diaper, we did it because that's what the baby needed. No questions; no whining. In fact, we *wanted* to do it because we loved that little bundle of flesh who came from *our* flesh, which motivated us to provide care.

And Jesus did that for us! He covered His divinity with our humanity, adapting to us, and dying for us in order to renew us to Himself. No questions; no whining.

It will require tremendous spiritual strength, though. Jesus got His strength through constant communion with God, using God's power. Likewise, you have to be that committed to the Lord for Him to give you the power to adapt to your mate.

This week's homework:

If you haven't done so already, take a personality, loving style, and spiritual gifts test. Together, take your results to a Christian counselor to interpret what they mean for your relationship.

WEEK 20

You're different enough to enrich each other.

"And he gave some, apostles; and some, prophets; and some, evangelists; and some, pastors and teachers; For the perfecting of the saints, for the work of the ministry, for the edifying of the body of Christ" Ephesians 4:11 & 12, KJV.

As Jackie and I were discussing this week's point with our daughter, she asked the question, "What do you say to the woman who feels like she has lost her identity in the care of her family? I'm talking about the woman who doesn't balance her role as wife and mother with her own personal fulfillment. And when the kids are grown and gone, she feels empty. Or how about the woman who begins feeling resentful that everything is about her taking care of her husband and children?"

My daughter's question follows a line of thinking that's similar to what I've heard some preachers' wives say. "Oh, I'm not a preacher's wife; I'm the wife of a preacher. I just married a preacher. That's HIS job."

The point this week is not talking about spouses creating separate identities and lives from each other. It's about bringing your individual talents and gifts to a marriage to feed the relationship.

I've never seen myself as separate from Jackie or my children. I see myself as part of the soil that helps him grow. I see myself as helping to mold other human beings in my family, to make each fit for God's kingdom. From that perspective, my role is vital.

Consider the Proverbs 31 woman: she's a homemaker; she's a realtor; she's a merchant; she's a clothing designer and seamstress; she's a philanthropist; she's an interior designer; and she's a wise counselor. She gets up while it's still night to provide for her family and employees, setting vigorously about her work, to achieve her goals.

Because of what she brings to the marriage and her family, her husband has full confidence in her. He has no worries as he fulfills his job with the elders at the gate. In fact, he *can* fulfill his duties, because his wife is fulfilling hers.

It's a trick of Satan for a woman to think or believe that because everything she does is benefitting her husband and children that she's losing her self-worth as an individual. In fact, it's just the opposite when you look back at the Proverbs 31 woman. It says that her children call her blessed and her husband praises her — not just within the household, but he brags about her to the other fellas at the city gate. And they all honor her for everything that her hands do. She actually gains self-worth through the work that she does caring for her family.

Once a couple marries, they're both agreeing to do everything to benefit the other through the strengths and gifts of their personalities, loving styles, spiritual gifts, and the knowledge and skills each develops along the way. This is how they, and their marriage, will grow together and prosper.

This week's homework:

After getting last week's results from your tests, sit and discuss how you already–and can–use each other's strengths and gifts to enrich your marriage and family relationships and activities.

WEEK 21

Recognize, appreciate, and use each other's skills to help love grow.

"As every man hath received the gift, even so minister the same one to another, as good stewards of the manifold grace of God" 1 Peter 4:10, KJV.

When our daughter married her husband, he had not finished college though he was working in a professional-related job. When she decided to get a master's degree in order to change careers, he supported her wholeheartedly, even though it meant leaving his full-time job and moving to another state.

As she went to school full-time, he worked through a temp agency because that was the only work he could find. Upon her graduation, they moved back to our city so she could begin teaching at her college alma mater. Again, he worked temp jobs until he landed a job at the same college where she worked.

Then, it was his turn. He took one class a semester until he could enroll in the college's adult and continuing education program. He received his college degree; and when he was offered the opportunity to go for his master's, my daughter, likewise, supported him wholeheartedly. She edited his research papers when needed, helped him study when needed, and prodded him and stepped back as needed.

When he failed his comp exam, prohibiting him from receiving his master's, she didn't berate him. She gave him space, let him re-group, and supported his financial request to go after it again. Now, they both have master's degrees. As they went through these challenges, their love for each other deepened because each worked for the other to help realize personal dreams and goals.

In last week's story of the proverbial wife, we read that she used all of her skills to support her family. This gave her husband freedom to develop himself to the fullest so that he became a renowned individual in his circle.

When you and your spouse can *recognize* each other's skills and abilities — the gifts God has blessed you with — and *appreciate* the value it brings to your

Recognize, appreciate, and use each other's skills to help love grow

family dreams and goals, you've made the first step in taking your love to the next level. People who feel affirmed and appreciated for what they bring to a job have no problem working hard because it helps everyone succeed. The same is true of marriage.

And don't determine the use of each other's skills by the traditional roles defined by others. The question is not, "Is this what a man is supposed to do or a woman is supposed to do?" The question is, "How can we use your skills to help you and the family flourish?" If she's good at managing money, then let her do it. If he's good at cooking, then let him do it.

As individuals, each of us has strengths and talents. When used to support your spouse, both you *and* your marriage will continue to grow stronger.

This week's homework:

Each of you create a list of strengths, abilities, and skills that you have been gifted with. Enumerate the ways that you can use what you've listed to support your spouse's dreams and goals. Come together and talk about your ideas and create a plan to achieve your goals.

WEEK 22

Frequent words of praise keep happiness and joy alive.

"A man hath joy by the answer of his mouth; and a word spoken in due season, how good is it!" Proverbs 15:23, KJV.

Have you ever seen a little boy who's trying his best to move some big object that's too hard to move — either because he's too little or doesn't have the strength to move it? All the while his father is cheering him on: "You go boy; look at you. Look at those muscles poppin'. You're doing it!" The boy strains harder and harder to prove his father's words true. When the task is complete, the little boy walks around with a self-satisfied look on his face because he did it (not realizing that his father was actually helping him)!

In Ephesians 5:25-28, the Bible specifically exhorts husbands to treat their wives as Christ treats His church, saying, "Christ's love makes the church whole. His words evoke her beauty. *Everything* he does *and says* is designed to bring out the best in her. And that is how husbands ought to love their wives" (The Message).

Genuine words of love and appreciation are primary tools that motivate women to give because affirming words trigger emotional satisfaction. A husband who talks to his wife in ways that build her up will reap the benefits of a wife who works hard to support him.

But although we often talk about women needing to hear words that affirm, don't think that men aren't interested in hearing words of love and appreciation as well. They may respond differently, but affirming words that build women up are just as motivating to men.

Genuine words of appreciation also guard against taking each other for granted. We know that going out to work every day, doing chores, and parenting the children is what we're supposed to do. But it still helps to hear that these things are noticed. The husband of the proverbial wife starting in verse 29 of Proverbs 31: "Many women have done wonderful things," he begins, "but you've outclassed them all!"

(The Message). And he goes on to shower her with more words of praise.

What happens, though, if one or both of you aren't big talkers, or weren't raised in a family where affirming words were demonstrated? You could start by thinking about specific things that your spouse does that make you happy, and turn it into praise recognition for her or him. You could also ask your spouse to tell you what you could say that would make her or him feel appreciated.

Once you get some answers, you will need to practice using affirming words, because it is a learned art. Oh, it will feel awkward at first — and it may feel and sound contrived. But the more you do it, the easier it will get. And Ephesians 5 says you'll get a good result, because God will allow that gift to develop.

This week's homework:

Begin a list of attributes your spouse has, or things your spouse does that make you happy or appreciative. Use specific words or language that describe your spouse as an individual; don't use words that generalize or stereotype. Then, set a reminder for yourself to praise your spouse at least once a day for something on your list.

WEEK 23

Daily demonstrate your love for each other.

> "Though I speak with the tongues of men and of angels, and have not charity, I am become as sounding brass, or a tinkling cymbal" 1 Corinthians 13:1, KJV.

Last week, we talked about the importance of building up your spouse with affirming words. But words alone don't work. Behavior supports what words say. The two must go together.

Many times, Jesus talked about the emptiness of words that is not matched with like behavior. In Matthew 25, He gave the story of separating His followers the same way that a shepherd separates sheep from goats.

Like sheep and goats, which both followed the shepherd, all the people claimed to follow Christ. What was the distinctive factor that made Jesus label one group "righteous" and the other not? What made Him put one group on His right and offer eternal life and the other on His left and sent away from Him? Their behavior. The righteous behaved in ways that satisfied the needs of others who needed help while the unrighteous did not.

I Corinthians 13 talks about the same thing — words that are empty because of no supporting actions. You can't just say, "I love you," and expect that to suffice. You have to show it through action. It doesn't have to be big, breath-taking action. It's action that the spouse needs to feel loved.

When we were counseling a couple going through some challenges, the husband — in response to a question — said, "I don't know what she wanted. I gave her money; I bought her everything she needed!" That's kind of a stereotypical attitude, right? Many husbands work hard to give their wives the big houses, the upscale cars, the clothes and shoes, and then feel as though that's enough for them to show their love.

What this man's wife really wanted was his time. She said that she was most happy when he picked up a dishcloth and began drying the dishes as she washed them. In response he remarked, "You mean all of this money I've spent on her and all I could've done was pay a dollar for a dishcloth and dry dishes for her?" Yep! Pretty much.

In other words, it's important to keep behavior priorities. Actions that don't define love the way your spouse defines it should not replace those that do.

That's what Jesus did for us. Christ didn't just say, "Father, I love them so much. I'm so glad We created them. Too bad it didn't work out." No! He demonstrated His love for us by giving up what separated Him from us, and becoming one of us. And eventually He gave up His life for us.

Love can be generated by appropriate behavior in accordance with what God has suggested in His Word. If we do this for each other, the bond of love will grow stronger.

This week's homework:

Like last week, begin another list — this time of behaviors that make your spouse feel loved. Whether you can observe specific behaviors that make your spouse happy or have to sit down and get ideas from your spouse, purpose to *do* something each day for him or her. Remember, it's not a competition but is showing love to your spouse in ways he or she enjoys.

WEEK 24

Motivate resolutions by never making divorce an option.

"And he saith unto them, Whosoever shall put away his wife, and marry another, committeth adultery against her. And if a woman shall put away her husband, and be married to another, she committeth adultery" Mark 10:11 & 12, KJV.

At the end of a weekend of seminars that we conducted at a church, a woman walked up to Jo. She took some papers out of her purse and showed them to her. They were divorce papers. "I want to thank you and your husband," she said, "for saving my marriage."

Motivate resolutions by never making divorce an option

Whatever that woman was experiencing with her husband, what we shared with her renewed her commitment to stay married and work on their relationship.

When the Pharisees asked Jesus about divorce in Mark 10, Jesus asked them, "What did Moses say?"

They answered, "Moses gave permission to fill out a certificate of divorce."

Jesus responded, "He only did it as a concession to your hardheartedness. In the original creation, God made male and female as an organic union — no one should desecrate His art by cutting them apart" (The Message).

Jesus' response sheds light on how sacred He considers the marriage vows. He never intended for couples who marry to divorce and then marry other people. In Matthew 19, Jesus told the Pharisees that the *only* exception for divorce, and subsequent remarriage, is adultery.

People often challenge that view by asking, "Well, what if you're being abused?" Or, "What if your spouse isn't a Christian?" Or, "What if your spouse has an affair?" Or, "What if your spouse wants to divorce you? Does God expect you to stay married?"

Because we are fallen human beings, there are many scenarios that challenge the marriage vows. No, God does not expect you to *physically* stay in an abusive marriage. But separation accomplishes that. Also, if a spouse insists on getting a divorce, agree to it; but you can determine to honor and abide by the marriage vow.

In any possible marriage scenario, the first option God *prefers* is forgiveness. That's what He does with us. The bible story of Hosea and Gomer is the living example of how God views His commitment to us, no matter how many times we reject Him.

We know this view is directly opposed to societal notions about marriage which say, "I will love you for as long as you treat me right and make me happy." But if you go into marriage thinking that if it doesn't work you'll just get out of it, odds are it won't.

Rather, if a couple agrees that divorce is never, or will never be, an option, you're pledging yourselves to doing *everything* possible to keep the marriage intact. This means that you'll behave in ways that will keep the relationship strong, or restore it if it weakens or breaks.

This week's homework:

Using several bible translations study the book of Hosea. What specific lessons are taught about commitment that challenge societal views about marriage and divorce?

WEEK 25

Listen… listen… listen to each other.

"Hear instruction, and be wise, and refuse it not" Proverbs 8:33, KJV.

Remember the story of King David and Nabal? Nabal was preparing a feast for his shepherds to celebrate the end of sheep shearing. King David sent his men to Nabal to ask that he share food with them as a thank you for watching over his employees while they were herding sheep through the wilderness. But instead of listening to them, Nabal insulted them, refused them, and sent them away. As a result, David and his men prepared to retaliate.

When Nabal's wife, Abigail, heard what her husband had done, she met David and his men with food and drink, humbly begging forgiveness and averting the household's possible destruction.

Not listening causes stress, frustration, anger, and sometimes, hopelessness — all of which damage relationships.

You and your spouse should work together to create an environment that promotes listening. You do this first by deciding that you'll do whatever it takes to protect and enhance your marriage. This mindset will help you to willingly recognize natural tendencies that make listening a challenge for you and will motivate you to change them.

As the listener, don't be quick to react to displays of frustration or anger, especially if the issue seems trivial. Realize that there's usually a deeper, unmet need that's driving the action. Rather than jumping to defend yourself or provoking more outbursts, ask questions and repeat the answers to make sure you're clear about what your spouse is saying and that you're rooting out the real problem.

As the talker, starting with, "You always…" is not the best way to express your need. A person who feels attacked will always throw up defenses which only block one's desire to listen. Talk about how a situation makes *you* feel, taking the focus off of your spouse and putting it on yourself, which helps to keep defenses down.

Jo remembers her mother saying how important timing was. Her mother knew how to pick the right moment to talk to her husband. It didn't matter if it were 2:00 or 3:00 in the morning; if her dad were relaxed and happy, her mom could use the right words to speak to him. If it's not a crisis, it's much easier to listen and talk about touchy subjects when you're feeling satisfied and close to your spouse.

Routinely "bathing" each other with those affirming words, especially when your spouse is "getting it right," will erase insecurities that challenge listening. If your spouse knows and feels that his or her actions meet your needs, it will motivate him or her to want to know how to continue.

Lastly, become proactive like Abigail. She didn't wait to see what the outcome with David would be. She disarmed him with humility and kindness. Disarm your spouse by asking how you're doing as a listener; ask how you can listen better. Then ask God to help you follow through.

This week's homework:

Write down your strengths and weaknesses as a listener, and your spouse's strengths and weaknesses as a listener. Using the tools described above, compare your reflections and discuss how they're similar and how they're different.

WEEK 26

Respect each other's needs and ideas as important.

"And the Lord was gracious unto them, and had compassion on them, and had respect unto them, because of his covenant with Abraham, Isaac, and Jacob, and would not destroy them, neither cast he them from his presence as yet" 2 Kings 13:23, KJV.

When two distinctly individual people come together in marriage, it's inevitable that two distinctly different views will vie for attention on some issues. From the trivial to the complex, you and your spouse may offer dissimilar ideas on how to solve problems or make decisions.

Respect each other's needs and ideas as important

How often this happens depends on how assertive or aggressive you are with giving your opinion. For some couples, it seems to happen all the time with anything. For others, it happens moreso for major decisions. Either way, the amount of value you place on your partner's ideas versus your own can set the stage for fireworks — either good or bad.

A person's ideas are important to him or her because, often, our ideas grow out of our personal needs or wants. So, it doesn't matter if our ideas seem wrong to someone else; they're right to us. For that reason, and building on the principles from the last five weeks, your partner's ideas deserve respect.

Respect — giving high regard to or for — means treating each other's needs and ideas as valuable. This actually reflects the high regard each of you holds for the other as an individual. If I value you, then my love for you makes me value what you offer to a discussion, especially if your ideas align with your gifts, abilities, and skills.

But what if the idea offered will do more harm than good; or, what if one can prove that one idea is just better than the other?

Respect doesn't mean agreement; it means not dismissing an idea because you don't agree. It means not pushing your ideas onto each other as the only way or manipulating each other to give in.

God didn't agree with Israel's desire for a king, but He didn't dismiss it, either. Neither did God agree with Israel's desire for meat when they got tired of eating the manna. In both cases, God tried to show Israel why both of those ideas would result in more harm than good. But when they insisted on their way, He let them do it their way — and they had to deal with the results.

Doesn't God still treat us that way? He — Who sees the end from the beginning; He, Who *knows everything*; He, Who created us — doesn't force us to do anything His way. Even though His way is *always* the best way, He wants our respect and love for Him — what He means to us — to be the driving force for our accepting His way.

Likewise, let the value you place on each other drive how you work together to make decisions.

This week's homework:

Take some time to analyze how you and your spouse make decisions. Is there a pattern to the process? How respected do you feel during the decision-making process? If there are times when you don't feel respected, what specific language or actions contribute to your feelings? Come together to compare and discuss your thoughts.

WEEK 27

Settle your differences by meeting each other's present needs.

"Let us therefore follow after the things which make for peace, and things wherewith one may edify another" Romans 14:19, KJV.

When Jackie and I were both working outside of the home, one of the morning chores was spreading our bed. I wanted the bed spread a certain way, and he wanted it spread a different way. However long the tension brewed, it got to the point that one morning we just walked away from the bed and left it unspread. Later, we determined that our relationship was more important than which way to put the pillows, and one of us deferred to the other.

How could something as trivial as how to plump the pillows cause such tension? Because what I was really fighting for, at that moment, was my need to be in charge — my need to feel equal to Jackie.

Most times, differences in ideas that turn into arguments between couples are driven by unsatisfied needs that each wants met by the solution. The argument ensues because one or the other doesn't believe the proposed solution will do that. Or, the topic of argument is a cover for something deeper.

If one spouse is more assertive and dominant in the relationship, the other often needs to feel respected or equal to that mate. If one spouse's ideas always seem to win out, the other often needs to feel recognized and affirmed for what he or she brings to the table. If one spouse seems to be involved in activities outside of the home or with other people, the other may need to feel included, or more of a priority.

If you find that discussions over issues — like our spreading the bed — often degenerate into arguments, take time to discover if there's a deeper need that you need to fill. When one of you can give way to the other for the sake of peace, do it.

What about arguments around situations that require major decisions? Should the one who argues with the best skill, or the loudest, win? Or should you agree to disagree and the wife defer to the husband as the head of the household?

We suggest that you both defer to God's model. Jesus' prayer for His disciples was, "Father, let them be one as we are one. I in you; you in me; and we in them" (John 17:21). That prayer reflects full agreement. But how do two human beings — who aren't God — come to full agreement?

In our seminars, when people couldn't agree, we suggested that we investigate, together, what God says He would do in such a situation and see which idea came into greater accord with His solution.

When you have a plan, and I have a plan, let God have the final say in helping you create a new plan that you can both agree on. The closer you come to Him, the closer you'll come to each other.

This week's homework:

For the week, keep a diary about arguments that you have had. When did they occur? Who was fighting the hardest for his or her way? What was your reaction, and why? At the proper time and using the proper language, come together to discuss your findings and to create solutions.

WEEK 28

Never go to bed angry.

"Be ye angry, and sin not: let not the sun go down upon your wrath…" Ephesians 4:26, KJV.

Over the last couple of weeks, we've been talking about settling differences. But, let's face it: some arguments turn into downright fights. Whether the fights are verbal or silent, if one of you is becoming angry and obstinate, something is wrong.

Psychologists see anger as a form of fear triggered by insecurities and unresolved issues in our lives. When we encounter behavior or responses that dredge up those feelings of fear over and over again, we display our displeasure through anger.

Our text this week acknowledges anger as a natural emotion. It starts off, "Be ye angry…" As fallen human beings, we are going to be angry at some point. Usually, we're most comfortable displaying anger toward those who are closest to us.

But the next phrase in the text is, "and sin not…" How can one be angry and sin not? Often, we go to the story of Jesus turning over the money changers' tables in the temple while wielding the whip as an example of being angry but not sinning. We call it "righteous indignation."

But if I get to a point where I believe that you are disrespecting my needs and constantly walking over them to satisfy your own, I'm probably not feeling what Christ felt. I'm probably feeling more like I need to get rid of you because I'm fearful that you'll never change.

"Be ye angry, and sin not" means that although I can't control how I feel, I can control how it manifests itself and how I respond. I don't have to allow my anger to drive destructive behavior. Instead, my goal should be resolving the issue that promotes my anger.

Now, what about the second part of the text: "let not the sun go down on your wrath." Is it realistic to think that anger should always be resolved before bedtime? What about the people who need a few days to process their feelings and views before they talk it out?

In that case, we say take it to the Lord. We don't realize the power of prayer as a relational tool. Pray for your spouse, in his or her hearing.

No, I'm not talking about, "Dear Lord. Help Jo to realize that my way makes more sense. Make her more willing to listen, and support me." This isn't about using audible prayer as a weapon to manipulate the other.

I'm talking about praying in a way that shows that you're sorry that your spouse is hurt and that you want to help: "Lord, I love Jo. I want her to be happy. Please send your Holy Spirit to enlighten us both so we can understand how to resolve this issue."

When you pray that way, you're showing how much you value your spouse and your relationship, and how much you want to serve him or her in a way that meets both your needs.

This week's homework:

Think about instances when disagreements or arguments have produced feelings of anger in you. Can you pinpoint the fear or insecurity that drove those feelings? How did your spouse heighten the fear or insecurity? What can your spouse do to alleviate the fear or insecurity?

WEEK 29

Unresolved anger and resentment will destroy a marriage.

"...Neither give place to the devil" Ephesians 4:27.

When Lucifer decided that, as the head angel, he was important enough to become God, he became very angry when God rebuffed him. As God and the other angels tried to reason with him and love him back into his assigned role, Satan sowed discord throughout heaven. When Satan's anger threatened to destroy God's government, God put him out.

Cain's jealousy, and ultimate murder of Abel, stemmed from his anger at God for putting his parents —Adam and Eve — out of Eden. He couldn't understand why God pronounced such an impactful curse on his parents just for eating a small piece of fruit. So he took his anger at God — for what He did to his parents *and* for not accepting his offering — out on his brother by killing him.

In both instances, we see how unresolved anger led to destructive behavior. That makes sense when we think about how anger stems from fear driven by insecurities, as we discussed last week.

Fear and insecurities compel us to protect ourselves — whether internally or externally. Internally, people protect themselves through denial, or numbing their feelings with substances, or closing themselves off from others. Externally, people protect themselves through denial, or willful ignorance, or lashing out at others. We see this behavior all around us more and more — a "get-them-before- they-get-me" mindset. Sadly, many people operate from that mindset in their marriages, giving Satan a foothold to use their anger as a tool to push them into destructive behaviors.

Do not let anger fester and build resentment toward you or your spouse. This is why we've spent the last three weeks talking about respecting and settling differences. If you allow negative feelings to build, you'll end with negative results.

We've given you several suggestions on how to resolve issues. But realizing that many issues reflect deep-seated needs, you must recognize and accept it when you can't do it on your own. Don't hesitate to use a Christian professional to help you. Remember, if your relationship takes priority, you'll do anything necessary to enhance or save it.

This week's homework:

Are there any issues in your marriage that cause heated arguments and never get completely resolved? These might indicate areas that are being driven by deeper problems than the topics you actually argue about. Analyze the issues that drive you to anger in your marriage, and pinpoint the fear and/or insecurities at the base. If that's hard for you to do, consider talking with a marriage counselor who can facilitate that process and resolution with you.

WEEK 30

Forgiveness and love will save a marriage.

"Then came Peter unto him, and said, Lord, how oft shall my brother sin against me, and I forgive him? till seven times? Jesus saith unto him, I say not unto thee, Until seven times: but, Until seventy times seven" Matthew 18:21 & 22, KJV.

Hot-headed, short-tempered, ready-to-fight Peter was not a person who let anybody get away with anything! He was all about defending himself, and anyone close to him, from any threat of harm. So for Peter to even consider forgiving someone who wronged him repeatedly was *huge*!

Forgiveness and love will save a marriage

It was so huge that he went to Jesus expecting a pat on the back for being willing to forgive seven times! To him, that was a big number, so forgiving that many times was sure to be Christ-like.

But Jesus said, "No, Peter. Forgive your brother 490 times. Four-hundred and ninety times?! Four-hundred and ninety?! Are you kidding? Who's going to count up to 490?

Well, that's the point. Jesus was saying there is no time that we shouldn't forgive someone for hurting us. And it's hardest to forgive those who are closest to us, especially our spouses. They're the ones that we shouldn't have to protect ourselves from. But often, they're the ones who hurt us the worse.

Through all of the differences, arguments, or destructive behaviors you and your spouse have experienced, forgiveness is *the* relationship fixer. The depth of love that you have for your spouse determines your breadth of willingness to forgive.

Forgiveness is an active mindset and behavior. Think of a physical wound or cut. It must be cleaned, soothed with a healing salve, sometimes bandaged, given time to scab over and for the scab to fall off on its own. It's an active process. Anything that interferes with the process delays healing.

Likewise, emotional wounds and cuts go through the same steps. They must be cleaned through issue resolution. They must be soothed with the healing salve of assurance, affirmation, and proof of change. They must be sometimes bandaged through self-protection and preservation. The more the offender does to actively prove that he or she understands the pain they've caused and are taking steps to make sure it doesn't happen again, the faster the wound or cut will scab. Once the scab falls off, the wound is healed forever.

If you, as the offended or the offender, are impatient with the healing process — saying and doing things to hurry it along because it makes you look or feel bad — you will delay healing. Patience is paramount to total healing as is prayer for God's help in giving it to us.

When you're tempted to rush the process, remember how often and how long God waits for us to "get it right." He's still waiting and forgiving. We should do no less than He.

This week's homework:

Assess your capacity to forgive. Is it hard for you to forgive? Are you vengeful or vindictive? Or do you forgive without expecting or demanding change? Do you forgive up to a certain point and then stop? Uncover anything that impedes your ability to forgive as God does, and seek resolution.

WEEK 31

Togetherness in work and play will keep you bonded.

"Again, if two lie together, then they have heat: but how can one be warm alone?" Ecclesiastes 4:11, KJV.

Jo and I *really* enjoy being together. We have lived our marriage doing pretty much everything with each other, whether the two of us alone or with others. If either of us had a working trip to go on, the other made arrangements to go along. With five children, we had to intentionally plan short, and long, get-aways in order to keep our bond strong. If people see one of us, they know for certain that the other is close by.

Some other couples seem to live life separately. We have literally seen couples in church where each spouse sits apart from the other. Other couples whom we know are married, we *never* see together. We also know couples who go to different churches; couples who vacation separately; and couples where one spouse is left alone while the other is always busy with some activity.

Couples have varying ideas of what "togetherness" means. Some may wonder, "Do we have to spend every non-working moment together? Is it wrong to socialize, or take trips, or relax without your spouse? After all, I see my spouse at home: we eat together, sleep together, and watch TV together."

Our daughter calls that "default togetherness." Because you're married, of course you'll see your spouse at home or in bed. But the "togetherness" we're talking about is intentional.

God made Eve for Adam because He knew that Adam needed companionship. He told Adam and Eve to stick together in the garden, in work and play, in order to be a stronger unit against Satan. God also said that married couples should leave their families and cleave to each other. The word "cleave" means to adhere firmly and closely and loyally and unwaveringly.

God's counsel suggests that His ideal is much more than default togetherness. He's built us to need human bonding, and that only happens through the time spent together. The more you do together, the stronger the tie becomes.

Togetherness in work and play will keep you bonded

We know that there are periods in life when work and children limit intentional togetherness, but it shouldn't be a preferred way to exist. We also know that sometimes you may want to socialize with girlfriends or guy friends. But again, if that's what you prefer in place of hanging together, it suggests that something is wrong.

It's dangerous to live life separately. It can give Satan a loophole to very subtly pull your marriage apart. Whether it's through diverging interests or other people, it's not healthy. Nor is it biblical.

The more intentional togetherness you share, the stronger your bond will become.

This week's homework:

With your spouse, compare how much default time versus intentional time you spend together. If the default time is greater, talk about the reasons, and make a plan for how you can increase your intentional togetherness.

WEEK 32

Make time to have fun together.

"A merry heart maketh a cheerful countenance: but by sorrow of the heart the spirit is broken" Proverbs 15:13, KJV.

When I married Jackie, he already had three young children, so it was important to us that we bond as a family. To that end, we initiated family night once a week. On family night we let the kids stay up late; we ate picnic foods; and we engaged in activities together. Sometimes we played games. Sometimes everyone had a paint-by-number set and we painted pictures together. Sometimes we did puzzles or watched family TV shows together.

Make time to have fun together

When Jackie worked as a dean of men for a dormitory of college and high school students, our family lived on site. When it was time for family night, he put an assistant dean in charge and ordered that no one ring our doorbell unless it were a dire emergency.

And because the job was so stressful and demanding, one weekend a month we packed up the kids and headed to a local hotel. There, we could just be together and have fun without distractions.

We also made time to have fun together just as a couple. When we began traveling to present seminars on married and family life, we always included time for fun. Over our years of meeting with and helping couples, God blessed us with resort trips, cruises, and beach trips, along with the regular stay-with-a-church-member trips. Wherever we were, we were able to keep our fire burning while igniting others.

And just about every anniversary, we left the children home and went to a hotel overnight.

When the business of living takes you and your husband and your children in different directions all of the time, it's hard to stay intimately connected. You start living as roommates, passing each other as you run here and there, fulfilling this obligation and that requirement. Soon, you don't know each other as people with goals, hopes, dreams, and interests beyond the routine. You lose touch with each other as individuals, which sets you up for growing apart.

Just like you make time to go to work, make time to attend church, make time to attend meetings for work and school, make time to taxi the kids around, and make time to take care of household business, you have to make time to have fun and relax. It will not happen on its own; you have to proactively plan for it.

Don't think that it has to always be a major trip somewhere. Weekly lunches, date nights, overnight or weekend excursions or "stay-cations," are just as effective. But when you can, take those major trips, too.

Today's text reminds us that feeling happy shows on our faces and through our behaviors. It's important to our overall health to enjoy each other through relaxing and fun activities. Yes, life is serious business — but so is the fun!

This week's homework:

Together, create a calendar of just fun activities. You choose the time increments of the calendar: whether monthly, quarterly, or yearly. Whichever you decide, schedule fun times that realistically work with the rest of your routine. Agree that — except for unforeseen emergencies — *nothing* or *no one* will interfere with your scheduled plans.

WEEK 33

Sex is for pleasure; as well as for intimacy and creating children.

"Awake, O north wind; and come, thou south; blow upon my garden, that the spices thereof may flow out. Let my beloved come into his garden, and eat his pleasant fruits" Solomon 4:16, KJV.

During a seminar discussion we were having at a church, an older man stood up and very proudly said, "My wife and I have been married for 60 years, and never have I once seen the nakedness of her body!"

I couldn't help but respond, "Brother, you don't know what you've been missing."

Clearly, that brother was not acquainted with today's text, nor even the entire book! He also must've never read Genesis 18:12 where Sarah said — in response to Jesus' proclamation that she would bear a child for Abraham — "After I am waxed old shall I have pleasure, my lord being old also?"

Throughout the Bible, the sexual intimacy of a wife and husband is used as a metaphor for God's desired intimacy with His church. Why would God do that if sex were only designed for the purpose of creating children? And why would He include Song of Solomon as one of the Bible's inspired books?

Song of Solomon is full of insights on the pleasure of sex, along with lots of tips for how to make it such. For instance, the chapters tell how the wife planned all day for her and her husband's sexual retreat. She prepared her body – bathed, lotioned, and was smelling sweet. The husband took her under the trees, and they were naked in the breeze. He stayed there all day and night. And they thought of old ways and new ways to make love.

When you study Song of Solomon and decode the poetic prose, that couple clearly pleasured each other sexually. They couldn't get enough of each other! But, don't mistake that to mean that married couples can do anything sexually that both consent to.

In 1 Thessalonians 4: 3-8, God says to stay away from sexual immorality, each of us controlling our own body in a way that is *holy* and *honorable*. We should not abuse our bodies through lustful passions the way people do who don't know God or His will.

Sex is for pleasure; as well as for intimacy and creating children

This clearly sets boundaries for what a Christian couple can do to enjoy sex. Knowing that God wants us to fix our minds on what is pure, noble, wholesome, and lovely (Philippians 4), we should not treat our bodies in any ways that dishonor God, the Creator of our bodies. God's Word should set our boundaries — not secular science, wisdom, or pop culture.

As such, over the years I developed a resolution for myself; there is so much that God has given me to enjoy with my wife that I would rather run the risk of doing less than I could, than run the risk of doing more than I should.

This week's homework:

To understand the importance of sex for pleasure and intimacy, use several bible translations to study the Song of Solomon, along with other resources like Tommy Nelson's *Book of Romance* or Daniel Akin's *God on Sex*. Compare the sexual activities that are common in your marriage, to the standard set in the Bible.

WEEK 34

Live within your means to avoid financial problems.

"No servant can serve two masters; for either he will hate the one, and love the other; or else he will hold to the one, and despise the other. Ye cannot serve God and mammon" Luke 16:13, KJV.

Because I already had children when Jo and I married, there was never a time when we could spend money freely. As our family grew to four boys and one girl, groceries became premium items, along with everything else that it takes to care for a family.

Live within your means to avoid financial problems

Thankfully, Jo brought to our family talents of thriftiness she learned from her mother. Whatever she could sew that would help to stretch our dollars, she did. However she could stretch the food, she did. Nothing was thrown away or went to waste.

Yet, we still had periods when money was extremely tight. I recall one time, Jo and I went to a card store. Instead of buying each other cards, she stood at one end and I stood at the other, picking out three or four cards. We came together, handed each other the cards we'd picked out, and read them — right there in the aisle. After reading them, we returned them to the shelf and walked out of the store, thanking each other for those beautiful gifts of words.

It was a blessing that Jo's and my philosophy of money were similar. But that doesn't always happen. If one's a spender and the other is tight-fisted, trouble will ensue. That's why couples should forthrightly discuss how to agree on a common financial philosophy. But be careful to base your philosophy on God's principles and not secular ones.

In a parable that Jesus told His disciples in Luke 16, He showed that His followers should not view or use money in the same way or for the same reasons that non-believers do.

Secular philosophy says that money defines success; money gives you status; and status gives you power. Without money, you're insignificant. So people work themselves into health woes, family woes, and personal woes trying to make that "buck."

God views money as a resource to further His work. In addition, He ties our ability to manage earthly wealth directly to our ability to handle eternal wealth. That's why He ends the parable with this week's text; we can't serve Him and money; it's one or the other.

Yes, we need money to keep us and our families healthy and safe. We also need money to minister to and serve others. But if we're consumed with making more money than we truly need, just for status or ego, then we have to ask ourselves, "Whom are we *really* serving?"

Couples have to find a way to live in financial harmony that reflects spiritual stewardship. It might require trial and error or sitting with a financial advisor, but it will definitely require study and prayer.

This week's homework:

Using several translations, study Luke 16:1-13 to discover God's philosophy about money. Also consider the rich young ruler's story in Mark 10:17-25. Compare your financial philosophy, as individuals and as a couple, to God's. Where can you agree to reflect His principles and how can you implement them?

WEEK 35

Use credit only when *absolutely* needed.

"Render therefore to all their dues: tribute to whom tribute is due; custom to whom custom; fear to whom fear; honour to whom honour. Owe no man any thing, but to love one another: for he that loveth another hath fulfilled the law" Romans 13:7 & 8, KJV.

We live in a society built on credit. The financial system is designed to require credit in order to transact business. One can't rent a car or a place to live without credit. The average wage earner can't get a loan for any large purchase without credit.

If you are not taught financial literacy in your home as you're growing up, you will probably go along with what society says: you need credit! It's convenient and affords the non-rich the ability to look as though we own the same high-quality things that the rich do.

Jo and I jumped on the credit bandwagon, not trying to look rich, but with our salaries and family size, sometimes it was the only way to resolve household or life issues. Sometimes we just got tired of always making ends meet and wanted to "treat" ourselves.

There was a period in our lives that whenever Jo said, "I like that," I would buy it for her. If I couldn't get it right away, I would plan for it and then buy it; or it would come in the mail for her. It gave me a certain kind of satisfaction knowing that I could give her things that she wanted. It manifested my male identity as a provider.

Or, we'd go into a store running a sale, and end up with more than we actually needed — like my penchant for buying a shoe style that I liked — in every color — ending up with five pairs instead of one or two, just because I had a credit card.

I was not a slacker; I paid on our debt each month, on time, without fail — until I got sick. Then, I had to give up all of the side jobs I'd retained after officially retiring, unable to work anymore. When

Use credit only when absolutely needed

that happened, I no longer had enough money to satisfy my debts. Therein lays the problem with credit.

Today's text cautions us to pay what is due to everyone and owe nothing to anyone. Even if you pay on your debt — as I did at first — you're not supposed to owe anyone anything — which was my plight once I got sick and couldn't finish paying the debt off.

While a credit card is convenient and useful, only use it as necessary, and charge only as much as you can pay off at the end of the month. If you don't have money in the bank to cover what you charge, you're only one crisis away from financial distress. God doesn't want us, or our families, to live on the edge like that.

If using credit promotes an attitude and mindset that results in wastefulness, selfishness, greed, or stress, take a step back and evaluate your spending habits. Remember, God asks us to handle our money in ways that honor today's scripture completely.

This week's homework:

Assess your spending habits and your use of credit. How easy would it be for you to pay your debts if you were hit with a crisis? If necessary, consider taking a financial literacy course like Dave Ramsay's *Financial Peace University.*

WEEK 36

Using cash is better than credit.

"If therefore you have not been faithful in unrighteous mammon, who will commit to your trust the true riches?" Luke 16:11, KJV.

Once Jackie got sick, we had to create a new mindset of "cash-only" living. We cut up all of our credit cards, except one for emergency use, and we've been primarily using cash only over the last 10 years. Amazingly, since living on a cash budget, we've seen just how much we've wasted in the past and how little we actually need.

For example, one time, Jackie needed a suit so we headed downtown to a clothing store having a huge sale — $500 suits for $200. And wouldn't you know it: Jackie couldn't find what he was looking for in the $200 price range.

A salesman came to us, asking if he could help us. We described the type of suit we were looking for, and he led us to a rack of suits in a $400 to $800 range. Knowing these were way out of our cash budget, I started making excuses to get us out of the store: "Mmm, I don't really like that color," and "No, I don't really like that style, but thank you anyway."

After leaving that store, we went to a thrift store and, lo and behold, we found a brand new — pockets still sewn up — name-brand suit in the style Jackie wanted, for $40. He even bought a shirt to match!

Living this way helps us lead a less stressful, more joyful life. It feels good to know that everything we have now, we actually own. If there's anything we need, we wait until we have the cash for it. We've gotten to the point that when we have to "do without" for a little while, it doesn't bother us as much.

Now believe me, it's taken a while for us to get there. We've all been so conditioned for convenience, instant gratification, and "keeping up with the Joneses." (Did you know that many wealthy people enjoy hunting for and buying high-quality items at bargain prices?) But learning to "do without" is actually what God expects from us.

Jesus' life on earth was hallmarked by self-denial and service to others. He had only what He needed — nothing more and nothing less. Although He lived on earth for a very specific purpose, His example is ours to follow. Because, though, bringing souls to Christ is not our only focus, as it was for Him, it should be our main one.

We should not be living our lives in this world and doing a little work for God on the side. It's just the opposite; we should be doing God's work as we live in this world on the side. That requires self-denial.

I can't think of a much better way to begin developing that mindset than living a cash-only lifestyle. It can help focus you on what is really important in your life, changing your priorities and making you more reliant on God.

If we're faithful with how we manage our money and lives down here, we'll receive true riches in heaven — more than we can ever imagine. And it will all be free of charge!

This week's homework:

Discuss what it would look like to move to a cash-only lifestyle in your home. How does the idea initially make you feel? What perceptions and attitudes about material things would have to change in order for you to do that? In what ways can you gradually move toward that goal?

WEEK 37

Budget a faithful tithe and offering to keep God's blessings flowing.

"Bring ye all the tithes into the storehouse, that there may be meat in mine house, and prove me now herewith, saith the Lord of hosts, if I will not open you the windows of heaven, and pour you out a blessing, that there shall not be room enough to receive it" Malachi 3:10, KJV.

As a little girl, I kept a tithe jar for any money that I received. Each time I got a dollar, I put a dime in my jar. I was very faithful putting my tithe aside and paying it in church. I was taught that God required us to pay tithe and I wanted to obey. As a result, I remember how I enjoyed God's blessings.

One time, however, I got some money and I didn't put my tithe aside. It seemed like I lost all of it. I remember that so vividly because as a youngster, I proved this week's text to be true.

Because God asks us to tithe, Jackie and I have always paid tithe first before spending on *anything* else. We did it when we were working and we do it now with our retirement money. And we've witnessed, first-hand, God stretching our money or opening up opportunities for us to get what we needed to care for our family. It happens that way because God designed it that way. He responds to our obedience.

Many people in the corporate world who don't call themselves Christians adhere to the tithe principle because it works. Paying tithe is God and man working together for man's financial well-being. As the line in a well-known spiritual song goes, "You can't beat God's giving…The more you give [to Him], the more He gives to you" (Doris Akers).

The opposite is also true. In Haggai, God warns us about the result of not giving Him His due. Talking to the Israelites He said, "Ye have sown much, and bring in little; ye drink, but ye are not filled with drink; ye clothe you, but there is none warm; and he that earneth wages earneth wages to put it into a bag with holes" Haggai 1:6, KJV.

Not giving God His due shows a lack of love for and lack of faith in God. And He will not reward that.

You may wonder what to do if your spouse was not raised on the tithe principle and has a hard time understanding the value of giving God first "dibs" on your money. I remember a couple where the wife was a tithe payer and the husband was not. She tithed whatever money she received and the Lord blessed her, which also blessed him.

Pray for the right time to share the value of tithing with your spouse — what it means to you and what it has done for you. If understanding is still lacking, ask your spouse to tithe because of what it means to you and out of love for you. If your spouse's response is negative, don't respond likewise. Just continue to be faithful to God's request, and pray that God will convert your spouse's heart.

This week's homework:

If you're not used to tithing, or struggle with consistently paying tithe, use a concordance to study the history of tithing in the Old Testament of the Bible ending with Malachi 3:8-11. Use several bible translations to get a full understanding.

WEEK 38

Friends outside the marriage should be friends of the couple.

"Wherefore they are no more twain, but one flesh. What therefore God has joined together, let no man put asunder" Matthew 19:6, KJV.

My first wife and I, as teenagers before we married, cultivated a close-knit circle of friends from church who hung out together. Several of us married from within that circle, deepening our connections through the years.

When my wife died, to them it was like losing a sister. After Jo and I married, she stepped into that close-knit circle of friends — my circle. Any awk-

Friends outside the marriage should be friends of the couple

ward feelings among my friends had to be processed and worked through because Jo was now my wife. Anyone who couldn't accept her couldn't stay connected to me.

We know that before marriage, many form bonds of friendship that play significant roles in their lives. And after you marry, of course you want to continue many of those relationships. For some, that may include people they used to date.

We don't see anything wrong with keeping your friends, even exes, as long as those friendships include your spouse. This also goes for new friends that you make individually after you're married. But realize, there's a difference between being friendly and being friends.

Friendships require commonalities and an investment of time. As a married person, your tightest bond should be with your spouse which requires the lion's share of your time and attention. If other bonds are competing, they will intrude upon and disrupt your marriage.

Today, disruptions come in many forms: face-to-face, the telephone, the computer, and social media. That's right! Facebook, Twitter, Instagram, and all of the various socializing tools at your fingertips are, sometimes, the worse culprits.

"But," you might say, "my husband/wife is o.k. with me spending time with my friends. She or he knows that this is how I unwind or relax." Just because your spouse doesn't object isn't proof that it's not an issue. Sometimes a spouse doesn't say anything so as not to come between you and your friends. But believe me: your spouse is discussing her or his true feelings with others.

As usual, let's take our cue from God. In Exodus, God says He's a "jealous God," demanding our full devotion. He wants our undivided time and attention; He can't share with other gods. When we try to juggle our time and attention, it endangers our relationship with God.

It's the same with human relationships. If you stay too involved with other people, especially past loves, without including your spouse, it will endanger your marriage. We should be just as vigilant about guarding our marriages from competing relationships as we are about guarding our relationship to God.

This week's homework:

Examine the amount of time that you spend socializing with friends, whether in person or in other ways, without your spouse. If it's greater than the time you and your spouse spend together, take steps to change that.

WEEK 39

Loyalty is to one's marriage and family.

"Therefore shall a man leave his father and his mother, and shall cleave unto his wife: and they shall be one flesh" Genesis 2:24, KJV.

You've heard the saying, "Blood is thicker than water." This infers that relationships with members of your bloodline — particularly your parents and siblings — are more important than any other. Many believe that blood family is more important than the spouse as well, especially when family disagrees. But that view goes against biblical philosophy.

Our text this week says that a man should leave his family and cleave to his spouse, becoming as one. In Week 31 we mentioned that the word "cleave" means to adhere firmly and closely or loyally and unwaveringly.

Unwavering means "*firm* in your opinion, decision, allegiance" (Webster). Loyal means "having or showing *complete* and constant support for someone" (Webster). That's what God says about your spouse; not your parents or siblings. So how does that look in practice?

Well, Jo came from a close-knit family, but she was also the apple of her daddy's eye. Many times, he'd call our house and the first word out of his mouth was, "Jo?" even when I answered the phone. No "Hello" to me or anything.

One day I finally said, "Hi Dad. I know Jo's your baby and all, but I'm a person too; you can address me."

When her parents moved to our city and we moved into a house next door to them, we exchanged copies of our house keys to use in case of emergencies. But Dad used our key whenever he felt like it, just unlocking the door and letting himself in.

One day, Jo came home, went into our bedroom, and nearly jumped out of her skin when she saw a person on the bed. It was her dad! Sleeping! At that point, he and I had a little talk, which Jo wholeheartedly supported. I almost asked for the key back, but instead I set some boundaries, which he honored with no hard feelings.

Loyalty is to one's marriage and family

What about when your spouse is clearly at fault or wrong in a family disagreement? Or, what if your family notices unhealthy behavior by your spouse towards you? How do you practice loyalty then?

First, pray for wisdom as you listen to your family's concerns, and use the Bible as the final word of truth. Then *you* — not your family — should discuss the issue with your spouse, using all of the principles we've discussed in past weeks. Together, come to a resolution and move it forward with your family. Do not allow your family to browbeat your spouse.

Also, don't put your family in the middle of your marital spats. Although it's natural to confide in family members, bad-mouthing your spouse will only cause them to form negative feelings and opinions that linger long after you've resolved the issue. That's unfair to both.

Safeguard the sanctity of your marriage and family by letting no one come between you.

This week's homework:

Examine instances when you have not supported your spouse in disagreements with your parents or other family members. How could you have handled it differently? Talk with your spouse and create a game plan for demonstrating loyalty to your marriage and to each other at all times.

WEEK 40

A happy home is where God-likeness reigns supreme.

"For I have given you an example, that ye should do as I have done to you" John 13:15, KJV.

From the discussion beginning in Week 1, we've shared God's principles of love and marriage; principles that we've used throughout our 50 plus years of marriage and shared with couples around the country. And we're not done yet; there's still a little more to come.

We hope that as you've been learning God's principles, you've also been practicing them all along the way. That's what this book is really about — practicing Christ's example of how to love.

While it's good to read instructions for how something works, you can't stop there. You have to follow them, as well. Likewise, God says if you follow His instructions for how to live as husband and wife, you AND your children will be happy.

We looked at that word, "happy," in Week 3. We talked about how it represents a state of satisfaction and contentment from obeying God. So in the context of your home, it means that you and your spouse's relationship is on solid footing; both of your needs are being met, and you're enjoying one another because you're loving each other God's way.

Hopefully, that's what you and your spouse are experiencing. If not 100 percent, then at least much better than where you began. If not, you might need to ask some questions like:

- Am I accepting God's principles or am I fighting to do things my way?
- Am I opening myself up to God's correction of my shortcomings, or am I willfully blind?
- Am I selfishly cherishing things that I don't want to give up?
- Am I slipping into old, counter-productive behaviors?
- Are situations making it difficult for me to follow God's instructions?

If you've answered "Yes" to many of the questions, you need a reboot. Go back to God and ask Him to fix *you*. Ask Him to help you willingly respond to His convictions. You can't demonstrate God's likeness in your home without the power and know-how of the One who made you.

It's never too late to take a step back, recharge, and pick up where you left off. As Ecclesiastes 9:11 says, the race is not to the swift, but to those who give it time. So it's not about if you've been able to practice all of the principles discussed up to now. The real question is, are you making strides every day by consistently working on loving God's way? Because that is the real key to a happy home.

This week's homework:

Assess the changes you've made in how you love your spouse. What's been the easiest change to make? What's been the hardest? Why? Where do you need to demonstrate more God-likeness? Choose one area at a time, asking for God's insight and power on how to love like Him.

WEEK 41

Remember – YOU are not the family.

"He that troubleth his own house shall inherit the wind: and the fool shall be servant to the wise of heart" Proverbs 11:29, KJV.

In Week 15, we discussed how the Godhead functions in a hierarchy — God the Father, God the Son, and God the Holy Spirit. Likewise, God designed the human family to function in a hierarchy — husband, as the priest of the home, wife, as his helpmeet, and children, as their offspring who are commanded to honor their parents.

The trouble with our attempts to function in a hierarchy, though, is that many succumb to an inherent temptation to treat the hierarchy as a dictatorship. Whoever is on top treats the ones below like subjects who exist to do their bidding. That perverts God's example.

We learned that the Godhead works in partnership — each One having a role yet deciding, moving, and completing activities together. Nobody goes off on His own to determine what everybody else is going to do and then orders it be done.

Let's apply that to the family. First, you can't be a family alone. Family means a *group* of people with common bloodlines, or convictions, or affiliations — whether living under one roof or separated. So, you didn't marry yourself; you married another person.

Because you and your spouse, and then children, live under one roof, each person feels the impact of the decisions and behaviors of the others. That's why it's important that everyone works together. Although Jesus is the Head of the church (hierarchy), He says, "Come now, and let us reason *together*..." (Isaiah 1:18). You're either making decisions as a couple or a family because sometimes it's appropriate to involve your children, too.

During our courtship, when we started discussing marriage, it was vital to us to receive the children's blessing. As the adults, it would've been our right to move forward without permission, especially because we both knew it was God's will. But a new wife also meant a new mother — which would directly impact the children's lives.

When the children were broached with the idea, two agreed to it right away. The third wasn't so sure and needed time to think about it. We gave him that time and, eventually, he told us it was okay: we could get married. Praise God!

But that provides another lesson. If disagreements exist in the family regarding how things are done, the ones in charge shouldn't ignore the feelings of the others. Our family routinely engaged in "family meetings" to air out issues and complaints. As long as everyone maintained respect for one another, everyone could honestly speak his or her mind.

Through your study of love over the past weeks, by now you know that if you're using Godly principles to manage your family, you will not operate the hierarchy from a self-centered viewpoint.

This week's homework:

Ask each person in your family to write down instances when one person acts as if it's "all about him or her." Choose a neutral time and place to discuss your findings together as a family. Map out strategies for changing that dynamic.

WEEK 42

Don't neglect each other as you care for the children.

"Let the husband render unto the wife due benevolence: and likewise also the wife unto the husband" 1Corinthians 7:3, KJV.

When counseling couples, we often heard fathers complain, "I feel like I'm not important to my wife anymore. I feel neglected." The mothers often responded, "I'm worn out by the time I finish work, deal with the kids, and take care of the house; I just want to fall into bed."

Children cause couples to make huge adjustments in their relationships. Instead of focusing only on each other, you now have to split your attention to include them.

God gifted women with more of a natural instinct to nurture and provide for children. That's one reason why many women get so absorbed in mothering. When a woman compares her helpless babies to her adult husband, she believes that he doesn't need, nor should he expect, as much from her as they do. But that's an unbalanced view.

In the text, Paul admonishes married couples not to withhold sexual intimacy from each other except by mutual consent for spiritual strength — not parental duties — because neglecting each other can open the door for Satan to play on unmet needs.

We can expand Paul's principle to include all forms of marital intimacy. Satan will stoke feelings of neglect into flaming attitudes that begin building walls between spouses. Then, he'll attack your vulnerability by sending people into your life who will eagerly listen to you and offer to fill the voids you have. One way to guard against that is for you to partner with your spouse in childcare.

Jackie got involved by changing diapers, giving baths, and sometimes taking the babies on car rides to make them sleepy. His help freed me to complete other household tasks or to take care of myself. But he knew to do that because he had already been a father.

Ladies, don't assume your husbands can tell when you're overwhelmed or overworked and know when to help. Nurturing is not their natural gift. So teach them by asking for help and specifically stating what you need — without attacking them.

Men, don't assume your wives can tell that you're feeling neglected. When they're multi-tasking, your silent treatment will not register in their brains. Jackie had no problems telling me what he was missing, which allowed me to plan for together time.

Planning becomes crucial for both of you if you want to maintain your relationship. If you schedule time together and work together, no one will be too tired to enjoy the other.

God made each of you the other's *first* priority, which children should not displace. You need the same love and care from each other as the children need from you. Maybe not to the same degree or level, but your needs don't disappear. Remember, you're vital to each other.

This week's homework:

Discuss whether or not you and your spouse feel put aside by the other due to focusing on your children. Create a plan for how you both can work together to ensure that you consistently make time to satisfy your intimacy needs.

WEEK 43

Parent your children together.

"And if a house be divided against itself, that house cannot stand" Mark 3:5, KJV.

Children are masters at learning the strengths and weaknesses of their parents and using that knowledge to their advantage. For this reason, it's important that parents are on the same page when it comes to how you parent your children.

When you marry, you bring your own upbringing paradigm into your new home. So either you'll parent your children the same way you were or you'll purposefully parent them differently. Either way, if you don't create a *new* paradigm with your spouse, you're in for trouble.

Both of Jo's parents nurtured, cared for, and disciplined her and her brother. Being a minister, her father was home a little more, and his personality was more open and fun-loving, making him the "easier" parent. But when Jo and her brother tried to ask him for something they thought their mom wouldn't agree to, his first words were, "What did your mother say?"

In my family, Mom was the caretaker because Dad was gone two or three days at a time working on the railroad. My mother, being very docile, didn't like confrontation, so her control tool was, "I'm going to tell your father when he gets home." Sure enough, when Dad arrived, she'd recite a long list of offenses that my siblings and I had committed that he had to discipline us for. This created fear in us and a dread of coming home in him.

In our family, our children got nurturing, care, and discipline from both Jo and me, although Jo took the lead as the caretaker, and I took the lead in disciplining, especially our sons.

For couples who are not on the same page with parenting or discipline styles, you will need to study and talk it out together. Remember that your model is Jesus and the principles He espoused, which include:

- Don't provoke your children to anger (Col. 3:21).
- Don't withhold correction (Prov. 23:13).
- A soft answer turns away wrath (Prov. 15:1).
- "Train up a child in the way he should go"
- (Prov. 22:6).

You should also study how your children differ as individuals and how you can consistently grow as a parent. I was not the same type of parent later in my children's lives as the parent I started out being. "One size fits all" does not apply to parenting.

Our goal as parents should be to mold our children's characters and desires to be Christ-like. Therefore, we must demonstrate Christ in all of our interactions with them. And when we get it wrong, as we will sometimes, we should admit it, ask their forgiveness, and keep at it. Just do it together.

This week's homework:

Take some time to analyze your parenting paradigm. Where does it come from? How does it affect your child or children? Compare and contrast it with your spouse's. If your differences cause friction, create a new paradigm.

WEEK 44

Children feel happy and secure when the parents are happy.

"And I will not be burdensome to you: for I seek not yours, but you: for the children ought not to lay up for the parents, but the parents for the children" 1 Corinthians 12:14.

You've heard the saying, "Children are like sponges." They soak up everything that they see and hear. That's how they learn, and the household environment is a primary field of lessons.

Children watch their parents and create their sense of stability and security from them. If your relationship with your spouse creates an atmosphere of

Children feel happy and secure when the parents are happy

joy in the home, the children will be joyful. If your relationship with your spouse creates an atmosphere of stress in the home, the children will feel stressed.

Your marital relationship also provides the first cues that your children use when relating to the opposite sex. When children see Dad pat Mom on the rump every now and then, or see them kissing and hugging, they're learning healthy behaviors that demonstrate love and romance. If that's what they see most often, they'll begin imitating that same affection with you. That's why little boys want to marry their mommies and little girls want to marry their daddies.

Likewise, if children see Dad and Mom fighting and hear them screaming, cursing, and name-calling, they're learning unhealthy behaviors that demonstrate anger and a lack of control. If this is most of what they see, they'll begin imitating these behaviors, as well, with their siblings or other children with whom they interact.

How you and your spouse handle conflicts and disagreements will either model positive resolution or resentment and retaliation. Couples who think children should never hear their parents disagree are really depriving their children of learning valuable lessons if you're using the techniques we shared with you in Weeks 27-30.

The tone of your relationship directly affects how children see themselves and what they believe about love and relationships. When parents separate or divorce, its impact on the children never goes away.

Today's culture tries to soften that reality or act as though it's not true. Having worked with many people who've been children of divorce, we know there's a wariness that sets in that's very hard to remove even once they become adults. They're always on guard of anything being said or done that increases their sense of insecurity, resulting in walls that are hard to break down.

All through the Bible, God says that each of us is responsible for the influence that we have on those around us. As parents, our influence directly shapes the type of people that our children will become. We should feel a sense of awe when we think about the magnitude of that responsibility. It should keep us in constant prayer and make us more determined to maintain a solid marriage.

This week's homework:

Have a conversation with your child or children to explore how *they* see your and your spouse's relationship and what *they* think and believe about it. Be willing to *accept* their perceptions and how they're impacted.

WEEK 45

Create family traditions to celebrate special occasions.

"Seven days thou shalt eat unleavened bread, and in the seventh day shall be a feast unto the Lord… Thou shalt therefore keep this ordinance in his season from year to year" Exodus 13:6 & 10, KJV.

Up until then, there was no greater special occasion than Israel's delivery from slavery in Egypt. To keep fresh the memory of God's strength in delivering them from Pharaoh, God commanded that they observe some traditions: eating unleavened bread for seven days; giving the firstborn of both man and animals to God; and, sharing the deliverance story within families, from generation to generation.

These traditions were designed to keep the memory of God's power and protection and love for them in the forefront of the Israelites' minds. That is the same reason you should create family traditions, too.

We have family traditions that began when our children were very young, that continue now — even though they're in their 60s, 50s, and 40s. Our oldest children's maternal grandmother — whom we called "Mama," — was known for her gingerbread, among other specialty foods. We took that idea of gingerbread and turned it into a birthday tradition. For each child's birthday, Jo made gingerbread and served it with flavored gelatin and whipped cream.

Another "Mama" tradition that we kept going was making fresh ambrosia for the holidays. Mama served it on Thanksgiving, but we served it with Jo's homemade sweet rolls for Christmas morning breakfast. When she was living at home, my daughter and I would stay up until the wee hours of Christmas morning, peeling and skinning oranges and grapefruits to mix with fresh pineapple, coconut, maraschino cherries, and orange juice.

My daughter has kept that tradition going through the years: whereas, I started using canned fruit when I couldn't peel and skin anymore. But when she and her family moved back into town, fresh ambrosia reappeared on Christmas morning along with Jo's sweet rolls.

Create family traditions to celebrate special occasions

Another tradition we had was welcoming the Sabbath on Friday evening with lit candles, soft music, and a worship program led by the kids. We would end worship by toasting each person's testimony of thanks with sparkling juice in wine cups.

All of these traditions, and more, gave our children something to look forward to. They also provided a unifying connection between the siblings to each other and them to us as parents. Today, whenever we gather for family reunions, we have a lot of fun, laughing and teasing each other as we recall the different traditions that we honored together.

When you create positive memories as a family, the memories last for a lifetime. So it's not surprising, when your children grow up, that they keep some of those traditions alive in their own families. This allows the legacy of family love to endure from generation to generation.

This week's homework:

If you don't have many, or any, family traditions that you observe, think of different ways that you, as parents, can mark special occasions with your children.

WEEK 46

Have morning and evening family worship.

"Train up a child in the way he should go: and when he is old, he will not depart from it" Proverbs 22:6, KJV.

Jo grew up in a family that worshiped together every morning and evening. She remembers worship as a fun and rewarding time that she looked forward to. My family was just the opposite. We did not worship together in the home at all. When Jo and I married, we decided to adopt her worship tradition.

Family worship is important for two primary reasons: training and insurance.

Have morning and evening family worship

We felt it was important to train our children to place God number One in their lives. Since He is the One Who sustains and strengthens them, regular worship was a way to acknowledge Him and to thank Him for giving us life. We wanted to demonstrate that God should have a position of utmost importance in their lives instead of a casual one.

Family worship is also like insurance. For a child of God, every day is a challenge. We have a strong enemy whose one goal is to destroy our salvation. Keeping the Lord actively with us is the only way to keep Satan in check. We wanted to fortify our children and ourselves with God's Word before going out to deal with whatever the day brought.

So every morning, at about 6:00 or 6:30, we woke up the children before the school and work day started, to listen to a reading and pray. We did the same thing in the evenings, at about 7:00 or 8:00, when we also added some discussions about what they'd heard.

Sometimes we achieved the fun, rewarding worships that Jo remembers from childhood, especially when we let the children lead out. Other times, we can admit, weren't as great. We see now that it's important to make worship age-appropriate as much as possible. This was most difficult for us when our children's ages spanned from teen to toddler.

Sustaining family worship also became difficult as the children got older. Schedules changed, with people leaving and coming home at different times; and as the children grew into young adults, they viewed family worship more as a requirement than rewarding. So our methods changed — from training to leading by example. We encouraged them to have private worship; sometimes, Jo stopped them at the door to pray with them before they left for the day.

As we look back, we see areas where we could've done a better job: this is common for parents to do. But we also see the impact of family worship on our now grown children as many of them engaged in morning and evening worship with their own families. That's a great consolation to us.

So though you may feel challenged, we encourage you to incorporate family worship into your daily routine. Ask God to give you methods and ideas that make it relevant and enjoyable for your children while teaching them the importance of keeping God first in their lives.

This week's homework:

If you don't have morning and evening worship, think of ways you can add it to your family's day. If you have older children, ask for their input on how to make worship a benefit for them.

WEEK 47

Daily Bible study together *and* alone is essential.

"Give unto the Lord the glory due unto his name; worship the Lord in the beauty of holiness" Psalm 29:2, KJV.

During his ministry, Jesus often went off alone to pray to His Father. Many times, this was after a long day of teaching and healing people or very early in the morning before His day's work had begun. An author of spiritual books, Ellen G. White, says that it was necessary for Jesus to withdraw from His daily activities to His secret place of prayer, to seek divine strength in order to accomplish His duties (Desire of Ages, p. 363).

As lowly human beings, we need even more strength than Jesus did to accomplish our work — as individuals and as couples. By now, after reading all of the tips through the previous weeks, you could be wondering, "How in the world can I do all of this? This is too hard!" You might have already gotten discouraged at some point, having tried to make changes but slipping back into old habits. This is what makes daily Bible study, both alone and together, so critical.

You've already experienced how difficult it is to blend two individuals with different backgrounds, upbringings, and training, into one cohesive unit. It's tough. To be a unit, you have to begin at the level of each individual; the reason each person needs to study the Bible alone. You need God's guidance to change those things about you that impact your relationship. Then, you need God's guidance as a couple to help you operate together.

"But how can I fit it all in?" you might ask, especially after last week's discussion about morning and evening family worship. It can feel overwhelming when you think about having to work, eat, sleep, study, exercise, socialize, unwind, go to church, and on and on and on. Jesus had only Himself, His disciples, and His ministry to focus on.

While that's true, it's also true that we make time to do whatever we *want* to do, especially if we see it as valuable and necessary. For me, as a mother of five children, a wife, a homemaker, and an employee — I knew there was no way I could do all of that alone. I needed my Creator's guidance, encouragement, strength, and comfort. Now, although the children are grown and gone and I'm retired, I'm the caretaker of my husband who's dealing with major health challenges. I still need the same support from God.

So I go to my "spot" early in the morning and talk with the Lord about me. It's important to have a place and time when you can study without distractions, both individually and as a couple. The places and times will probably change through the years, but solitude is critical.

Jesus couldn't do anything without His Father's power. Neither can we. If you sense your need for God's help and you want to follow Jesus' example, He will show you how to carve out time to spend with Him together, and alone. Just know that the devil will do everything he can to discourage you, but God will help you succeed.

This week's homework:

Analyze your daily schedule and routines to see where you can carve out time for individual and couple study. Once you figure it out, commit to following through every day.

WEEK 48

As a wife, make Proverbs 31:10-31 your daily goal.

"Who can find a virtuous woman? for her price is far above rubies...Her children arise up, and call her blessed; her husband also, and he praiseth her" Proverbs 31:10 & 28, KJV.

In Week 20, we introduced the Proverbs 31 woman as someone who enriches her husband and children with all of her gifts and talents. Just like young people have celebrities that they copy, the proverbial woman is mine. To me, she's awesome.

At first glance, she seems superhuman. The list of what she does appears impossible to achieve. As we discussed this tip, my daughter said, "There's no way I could do all of that. It doesn't even seem like she sleeps more than a couple of hours. I need at least seven!" I have to agree; she does seem too perfect to be true, but she's supposed to be. God doesn't give us imperfect models to follow.

What I admire most about her is that she demonstrates the essence of God — selfless love. God the Father sacrificed His Son for me; Jesus put Himself completely aside to restore me to His Father; and the Holy Spirit constantly draws me to God.

Likewise, the proverbial woman puts herself aside to care for her household; she affirms her husband whenever possible without demanding anything from him; and she keeps her family running smoothly and efficiently. So, how can we be like her?

First, realize that she doesn't do everything described, every single day. She's a composite of virtues, not a list of daily activities. But she accomplishes all that she does through her spiritual connection, time management, and efficiency. For me, that means having my alone time with God, writing down "to do" lists to stay on track, and preparing what I can the night before.

Second we have to *want* to be like her. If she is who God holds up as my model, and I want to be who God asks me to be, then I want to be like her. Often when I think, "God *chose me* for this job!" I feel confident that I can do it.

Third, we have to know our personal worth. Not only did Jesus die for *me*, which makes me valuable, but also He's blessed me with skills, abilities and gifts that benefit my family.

Last, we have to *believe* that we can be like her. If God made her and me, and if God could speak something into existence from nothing, then I know He can help me handle my little stuff and achieve her example.

Yes, all that we do gets tiring, challenging, and frustrating; but, don't stay in those feelings. Remember, you're not trying to do everything every day. Make goals, and work toward one or two at a time using God's power to fuel you — knowing that God has chosen you; and believing you *can* become the proverbial woman.

This week's homework:

Using several bible translations and a concordance, study Proverbs 31:10-31. Dissect the proverbial woman's characteristics and virtues. Discover practical applications and gain support through the Proverbs 31 Ministry website and radio segments.

WEEK 49

As a husband, make Ephesians 5:25-29 your daily goal.

"So ought men to love their wives as their own bodies. He that loveth his wife loveth himself" Ephesians 5:28, KJV.

Men often like to talk about being the "Priest" of the house, or the "head" of their wives and families as a badge of authority. Many use the biblical command for wives to "submit to their husbands," as a dictate for male supremacy, or the idea of women being "weaker vessels" as a right for them to dominate.

Society bought into these distorted views giving rise to feminism. Who can really blame women for revolting against abuses and inequities they've endured as a result of these misinterpretations?

This week's passage begins, "Husbands, love your wives, even as Christ also loved the church, and *gave Himself up for it* (Eph. 5:25, Amplified). Just that last part alone counters all the distorted views about the male role.

Christ's entire focus was on loving the church back to God the Father. Christ met people's every physical, emotional, and spiritual need to the point that wherever He went, people thronged around Him. Those who received Him were completely changed. Then, Christ offered up Himself to be beaten, spit on, humiliated, and hanged on a tree for sins He didn't even commit — our sins that *we* should've died for.

So when God says that I should love my wife as He loved the church, He means that I should be meeting all of my wife's physical, emotional, and spiritual needs, willingly putting myself aside for her wellbeing — not the other way around.

Jo's become that proverbial woman discussed last week, and I've had a major part in helping her. I've always given her whatever she's needed to complete her tasks — whether equipment, money, encouragement, compliments, or my assistance filling in whenever she needed me to, it's always been my goal to help her to be who God has called her to be. Just as the proverbial woman's husband praised her, I've always publically affirmed Jo, especially to our friends, about the great wife that she is.

This week's text says that men should love their wives as their own bodies. That means you should seek for your wife the same comfort that you seek for yourself in any given situation. Every day your question should be, "What can I do for my wife that will make her feel fulfilled as a woman?" Every day your aim should be to demonstrate your answer through uplifting words and behavior.

If you love your wife the way Christ tells you to love her, you will reap the benefits. There's nothing that she won't do for you. She won't mind "submitting" or letting you fill the role of "priest" or "head of the house" because she knows that she is your first priority, and she trusts you because your words and behavior show that you've got *her* best interests at heart.

This week's homework:

Using several bible translations and a concordance, study this week's passage. If you're open enough, ask for your wife's feedback as to how your behavior compares to God's model.

WEEK 50

Make God your partner, and ask Him to help you love your spouse.

"Come unto me, all ye that labour and are heavy laden, and I will give you rest. Take my yoke upon you, and learn of me; for I am meek and lowly in heart: and ye shall find rest unto your souls" Matthew 11:28 & 29, KJV.

I remember it so vividly. Jackie was in graduate school full-time, working full-time, and parenting full-time. While he focused on studying and writing research papers, I focused on caring for the children and the house. At the end of the day, I was completely worn out.

Make God your partner, and ask Him to help you love your spouse

On one particular evening, I was standing at the kitchen sink when Jackie came home. As usual, I was extremely tired. So when he indicated that he wanted some intimate time, my spirits sank. At that point, intimate time was nowhere on my "to do" list. But my husband needed me. Because the Bible admonishes couples not to withhold sex unless both agree, I wanted to follow God's counsel.

I closed my eyes, right there at the sink, and breathed a prayer, "Dear Jesus, I want to love my husband tonight and give him what he needs. Please give me the energy to do it." And He did.

All of the love principles that you've studied throughout this devotional is what God requires us to practice. Because He requires it, He has to enable it. I — we — can't do it alone. This is especially true when couples are not on the same page.

If one of you has been reading this book and performing the homework and the other hasn't, you will definitely need God's power to help you *want* to follow through and do it, even if your spouse does not. If one of you doesn't see any need to change what you say or do in your relationship, the other will definitely need God's power to stay self-focused and change what He convicts you about.

You'll also need God's power to practice patience with each other as you work together to strengthen your marriage. He promises to give you that power if you ask.

In this week's text, God says, "Take my yoke upon you." A yoke is a wooden bar attached around the necks of two work animals so they can pull a heavy load together. That is what God is inviting us to do: attach ourselves *with* Him, so that the two of us — the two of you — can pull the heavy load *together*.

When you partner with God, whatever God asks you to do, you can expect to be able to do it. The question you must ask of yourself is, "Do I *want* to please the Lord in this situation? Or, do I want to please *myself?* If you decide to please God, you can rest because you know that He will give you whatever you need to follow through.

This week's homework:

By this time, you should know where you struggle the most to practice God's love principles. Specifically make a list of where you have difficulties; ask God to partner with you to overcome them; and, search the Bible for a promise you can lean on for each difficulty to remind you that God's with you.

WEEK 51

Recognize that love, marriage, sex, and family are God's idea — not man's.

"There is a way which seemeth right unto a man, but the end thereof are the ways of death" Proverbs 14:12, KJV.

When you look at the story of creation, particularly the part where God creates Eve, you'll notice something very interesting. First, let's put it into context.

God creates Adam and puts him to work. As Adam is naming the animals, he notices that each one is paired up. But he doesn't have anyone like himself, for himself. He mentions it to God. God says that Adam's right. *God* says, "It's not good for man to be alone; I will make a helpmeet for him" (Gen. 2:18). Then He puts Adam *to sleep* and creates Eve. When God presents Eve to Adam, *God* says, "A man should leave his father and mother and cleave unto his wife" (Gen. 2:24). *He* also tells them, "Be fruitful and multiply, and replenish the earth" (Gen. 1:28).

Nowhere in this account do we ever read about Adam giving God suggestions on how to solve Adam's issue. God took Adam completely out of the equation while He made someone suitable for him. Then God gave them conditions for happiness: Stay together; resist the devil; and obey Me. This account suggests a couple of things: 1) It's God's responsibility to choose a mate for each of us; and 2) If we follow God's plan and commands, we'll be happy.

Well, Jo certainly followed #1. While she enjoyed dating and getting to know the guys she went out with, she asked God to choose her husband. This freed her up to focus on developing herself as a woman and as a relationship partner. Once God put us together, we've both been striving for over 50 years to follow #2.

Yet, many people get their picture of happiness from the television, or news media, or social media. But if those pictures contradict what the Bible says, then your picture is coming from man, not God.

Man had nothing to do with creating the ideal. So why, then, are we so comfortable following what humans say about love, marriage, sex, and family

Recognize that love, marriage, sex, and family are God's idea — not man's

instead of what God says? Why are we so comfortable altering God's design to suit our own?

It started with "that tree." God told Adam not to go near the tree of the knowledge of good and evil. Adam didn't know why God commanded that; but, God knew that the mixture of good and evil would destroy His ideal. Satan appealed to Eve's pride which caused her to doubt God and assume that she knew best. We still succumb to that today.

What we hear humans teach is often a mixture of good and evil, which always causes problems. Just as God's beautiful creation instantly changed when Adam and Eve sinned, the same happens today. When we mix a little human perspective with God's perspective, it taints the entire view. That's exactly what Satan wants.

This is why we've deliberately used a biblical view for sharing what makes a marriage successful. All we have to do is decide to follow it and repel the urge not to.

This week's homework:

Look back through the homework assignments you've completed over the year, and record the impact of following God's design vs. man's design for love, marriage, sex, and family.

WEEK 52

Become a professional lover through study, time, and effort.

"Consider what I say; and the Lord give thee understanding in all things" 2 Timothy 2:7, KJV.

We've come full circle, back to the beginning of this book. In the Introduction, we said that becoming a professional lover — God's way — would take a commitment to study, time, and effort.

You've spent the last year studying God's blueprint for what's required of a professional lover. Although you've reached the end of this book, your study is not over.

Become a professional lover through study, time, and effort

As long as you're married, you'll be in marriage school — you'll never graduate. You are an imperfect person who married another imperfect person. Now that you've discovered the secrets for a successful marriage, you'll spend the rest of your time growing and maturing in your knowledge as you move through all of life's stages. That will require additional study and revisiting what you've already learned. After 50 years, we're still learning, not only because we're in a different stage but because — at this point in our lives — we're always forgetting.

You do reach a point, though, if you've truly studied, when all of this begins to make sense. For instance, most of what you've accomplished this year came out of understanding what love is, what it means, and what one does to love properly. You've learned some basic principles that apply to everything. As you practice them consistently, the pieces will begin to fall into place.

Other principles that you've learned, though, will take more time to perfect. We're constantly fighting against our human imperfections, including thinking we know it all or have better ideas of what to do, or listening to other imperfect people who think they have the answers. As such, it will take effort and practice to override our natural habits in order to accept and proficiently do what God asks.

Also realize that there is no set timetable for this, so don't require one for your spouse or yourself. You may not have even gotten comfortable, yet, disclosing your imperfections to your spouse or children (although, believe me, they already know them). While you don't want to put pressure on yourself, you do want to keep progressing. Don't use the fact that this is a complex process as an excuse to stagnate. Be steady in your growth.

Keep this book close; you might even re-read it. God's Word is so rich with lessons and truths that it's impossible to get everything the first time. We're sure that as you keep studying the passages in different weeks, you'll discover more and more information — with the Holy Spirit's help.

We're praying that the results you experience will afford you a marriage that exceeds your wildest dreams as you professionally love each other, together.

This week's homework:

Start over at Week 1!

www.ingramcontent.com/pod-product-compliance
Lightning Source LLC
Chambersburg PA
CBHW021952290426
44108CB00012B/1033